Kent Smugglers' Pubs

*To my wife Carol who now knows more about Kent Smugglers'
pubs than she ever knew she wanted to know*

First published in 2014
Reprinted 2015 and 2017
New edition, revised 2021
Copyright © 2021 Terry Townsend

Every attempt has been made by the author and
publisher to secure the appropriate permissions
for materials reproduced in this book. If there has
been any oversight we will be happy to rectify the
situation and a written submission should be made
to the Publishers.

A CIP catalogue record for this book is available
from the British Library.

ISBN: 978 0 85710 128 0

PiXZ Books
Halsgrove House, Ryelands Business Park,
Bagley Road, Wellington,
Somerset TA21 9PZ
Tel: 01823 653777
Fax: 01823 216796
email: sales@halsgrove.com

An imprint of Halstar Ltd, part of the Halsgrove
group of companies. Information on all Halsgrove
titles is available at: www.halsgrove.com

Printed and bound in India by Parksons Graphics

**Terry Townsend's other Halsgrove titles
include:**

Once Upon a Pint

*A Readers' Guide to the Literary Pubs & Inns of Dorset
& Somerset*

Bristol & Clifton Slave Trade Trails

Jane Austen's Hampshire

Jane Austen & Bath

Jane Austen's Kent

Wiltshire's Haunted Pubs & Inns

Pints & Pulpits – Devon's Historic Church House Inns

Dorset Shipwreck Stories – A Coast Path Guide

Smugglers Pubs Series

Kent Smugglers' Pubs

Dorset Smugglers' Pubs

Hampshire Smugglers' Pubs

Isle of Wight Smugglers' Pubs

West Cornwall Smugglers' Pubs: St Ives to Falmouth

*East Cornwall Smugglers' Pubs: Kingsand to
Mevagissey*

Suffolk Smugglers' Pubs

East Sussex Smugglers' Pubs

More Dorset Smugglers' Pubs

East Devon Smugglers' Pubs

Kent Smugglers' Pubs

Terry Townsend

CONTENTS

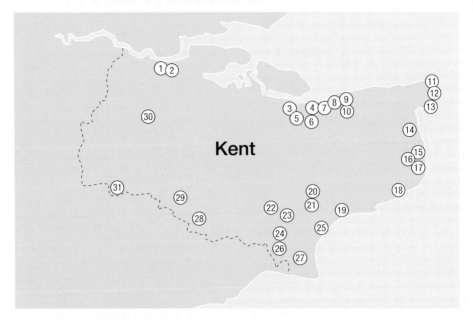

Kent

(1) Gravesend: *The Three Daws*
(2) Denton Wharf: *The Ship & Lobster*
(3) Conyer Creek: *The Ship Inn*
(4) Hollowshore: *The Shipwright's Arms*
(5) Faversham: *The Bear Inn*
(6) Faversham: *The Anchor Inn*
(7) Seasalter: *The Oyster Pearl*
(8) Whitstable: *The Old Neptune Inn*
(9) Herne Bay: *The Ship Inn*
(10) Herne Village: *The Smugglers Inn*
(11) Kingsgate: *The Captain Digby*
(12) Broadstairs: *The Tartar Frigate*
(13) Pegwell Bay: *The Belle Vue Inn*
(14) Sandwich: *The Kings Arms*
(15) Deal: *The Kings Head*
(16) Deal: *The Ship Inn*

(17) Deal: *The Royal Hotel*
(18) Dover: *The White Horse*
(19) Hythe: *The Bell*
(20) Mersham: *The Farriers Arms*
(21) Aldington: *The Walnut Tree Inn*
(22) Woodchurch: *The Six Bells*
(23) Warehorne: *The Woolpack Inn*
(24) Snargate: *The Red Lion*
(25) Dymchurch: *The Ship Inn*
(26) Brookland: *The Woolpack Inn*
(27) Lydd: *The George Hotel*
(28) Hawkhurst: *The Oak & Ivy*
(29) Goudhurst: *The Star & Eagle*
(30) Wrotham: *The Bull Hotel*
(31) Groombridge: *The Crown Inn*

In this new amended edition of *Kent Smugglers' Pubs* I have added a couple of entries that didn't make the short list the first time round: The Three Daws at Gravesend and The Ship & Lobster at Denton. I have also included The Crown at Groombridge which although it features in my forthcoming West Sussex book is actually just over the border in Kent.

I have deleted The Blue Anchor at Ruckinge which has sadly closed and also omitted The Royal Oak at Brookland which, as I write, seems to be facing an uncertain future.

I am happy to have the opportunity to respond to a couple of the readers who wrote favourable reviews even though one highlighted an error and the other an omission. A Romney Marsh farmer's wife good humouredly pointed out I had photographed *'the wrong type of sheep…unless they had soot on their faces!'* (see page 96). The addition of a map in this edition is the result of a suggestion from another reader and it's something I now include in all my books.

I have removed references to landlords, landladies and their staff because today many pubs seem to change hands with frequent regularity. However, even new landlords cannot change the stories behind the pubs themselves. In 1872 politician Sir William Harcourt observed: 'As much of the history of England has been brought about in public houses as in the House of Commons'. If you know where to look, and what to look for, a smugglers' pub will reward you with a wealth of history for free.

Terry Townsend

Terry Townsend, Somerset 2021.

INTRODUCTION

By the year 1200, England had become the largest producer of the highest quality wool in the world. The raw product was eagerly sought by continental weavers and in 1203 King John imposed a tax on its export. Soon afterwards an import duty was imposed on wine, cloth and leather entering the country. From the moment these taxes were imposed they were evaded and so began the delicious deception of smuggling.

It is a common misconception that smuggling was confined to Cornwall. In practice, Kent's proximity to France, established it as the main gateway for contraband. And, to the north-west of the county, England's capital beckoned with its voracious market for all things illicit.

Kent also had a large number of suitable landing places all around the coast plus a legion of sailors, boat builders and fishermen to provide the skilled men and vessels for the shipping. Inland people from every walk of life

Kent had a large number of suitable contraband landing places all around the coast.

OGDEN'S CIGARETTES

THE SURPRISE

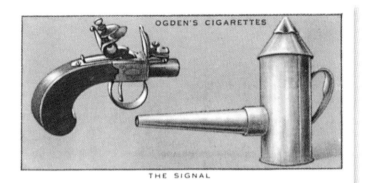

THE SIGNAL

The pan of a flint-lock pistol was used to flash a warning. A lantern with a long funnel could pinpoint a light in a desired direction.

became involved in hiding, transporting and marketing contraband goods. Young and old, men and women, farmers, agricultural labourers and pub landlords all played their part.

Support for smuggling extended to churchmen, magistrates and the aristocracy who frequently connived in buying contraband, financing smuggling operations and protecting smugglers from the law.

As the years passed England became involved in a succession of foreign wars that required funding. New duties were imposed on a huge range of items that all became targets for

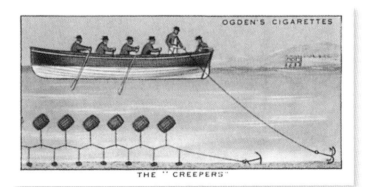

THE " CREEPERS "

All sorts of ingenious hiding places and practices were devised.

smugglers. The illegal trade flourished because the majority of the people did not consider it a crime. Indeed, at a time of widespread poverty in the rural south it provided a lifeline for some and an opportunity to get back at an unjust and unfair society.

Smugglers' trails were established where men and packhorses trekked through long nights under the weight of sacks of tea and barrels of spirits. All sorts of ingenious hiding places were made available along the routes in dugouts, stow-holds, barns, hayricks, coach houses, churches and the cellars and outbuildings of pubs.

Smuggling grew to massive proportions. It has been estimated that from 1700 to around 1850 a quarter of the country's import/export trade was illegal. The figure of the smuggler has provided material for innumerable fictional tales of intrigue and high adventure. In reality the law-makers had unwittingly created a climate in the country for the establishment of serious organised crime. The events which actually occurred in the heyday of smuggling provide us with stories every bit as wild as those that can be imagined.

Tangible links with this violent period are scarce, though there are some artifacts in a few museums. What has

Riding Officers were generally ineffectual in combating smuggling.

OGDEN'S CIGARETTES

THE RIDING OFFICER

survived are the many authentic smuggling pubs. In most cases the local inn became the centre of operations for the smugglers where plots were hatched, arrangements made and runs commissioned. The smugglers' pub served as a meeting place, recruitment centre, secret storage facility, distribution depot and valued customer.

Below left: Inland people from every walk of life became involved in hiding, transporting and marketing contraband goods.

Larger inns sometimes incorporated court houses; with gibbets and even gallows outside. Many pubs acted as temporary mortuaries and became emergency field hospitals where, after one of the numerous battles, injured smugglers and Revenue men were treated. Today, these old buildings with their low ceilinged bars, high-backed settles, flagstone floors and secret hiding places are where you must go to get a feel or understanding for the desperate days of the free traders.

Below right: Dragoons were sometimes called in to assist in chasing and apprehending smugglers.

OGDEN'S CIGARETTES

THE TUB MAN

OGDEN'S CIGARETTES

THE DRAGOON

Legends and traditions about smuggling abound. Favourite stories of how the local community out-foxed the Customs Officers have been repeated and embellished over centuries. Tales of hidden tunnels leading from one pub to another or from the pub to the church are still readily repeated. There is some evidence for a number of these claims but in reality smuggling became a brutal life and death game.

Through most of the smuggling history the free traders had it pretty much there own way. Preventative measures were poorly organized, under staffed and under funded. By the time of the Napoleonic wars Kent had developed into a bloody battleground of civil unrest. Notorious smuggling gangs formed in a number of villages under charismatic fearless leaders. These men were able to muster horses, carts, packponies and hundreds of helpers at short notice when a contraband run was imminent.

The crisis came to a head following the battle of Waterloo in 1815. The ending of the Napoleonic War brought the discharge – and therefore unemployment – of about 330,000 soldiers and sailors. This meant good recruiting opportunities for the smuggling gangs but it also meant a military force could now be made available to focus its attention on crushing the wicked trade.

In 1816 the Navy set up a 'coastal blockade' of armed sailors and marines on foot patrol. The smugglers' answer was to form in ever larger groups of 200 or more, protected by armed guards. The scene was set for some of the bloodiest conflicts.

Because smuggling became so entrenched throughout Kent, almost every pub at some time or another had an involvement. The collection featured here all have a documented association with smuggling. Wherever possible, I have chosen pubs that would still be recognizable to the 'gentlemen of the night' who frequented them all those years ago.

Gravesend
The Three Daws

6 Town Pier, Gravesend DA11 0BJ Tel: 01474 566869

www.threedaws.co.uk

Enduring for more than 450 years by the river's edge at the foot of Gravesend's narrow cobbled High Street, the wonderfully preserved Three Daws Inn continues to stand sentinel at the entrance to the famous pier. This ancient tavern, which served for centuries as a home from home for Thames river pilots was a haunt of smugglers and was regularly raided by the old naval press gangs.

William Shakespeare was just a year old in 1565 when the pub opened. Before that the building existed as five cottages constructed from locally-cut timber by unemployed ships' carpenters. There were no plans; windows, doors and beams were simply made to fit as the work progressed. The result was an ideal house for hide and seek. It had eleven bedrooms connected by five staircases.

The historic river scene at Gravesend pier.

The rambling old inn with eleven bedrooms connected by five staircases was an ideal house for hide and seek.

Situated at a strategic point on the river front and by the old Dover road, The Three Daws was an ideal location for smugglers who took full advantage of the cellars which run underneath the whole of the house. There were three secret tunnels that ran from behind the chimney breast to The Fisherman's Arms, out to the wharf and to St George's church. In March 1780, after a running battle in West Street between smugglers and Customs Officers, 80 gallons of Geneva gin were discovered in one of the tunnels.

The building existed as five cottages constructed by unemployed ships' carpenters before Shakespeare was born.

In 1798 when press gangs were looking for men to join Nelson's Navy the following order was issued by the Admiralty: *'The Three Daws is never to be raided by a press gang except if there are two, as so many seamen escape through its tortuous passages'*.

In 1962 when landlord Albert Kite undertook some repair and renovation work at the inn he discovered two rooms he didn't know existed; one was on the first floor and the other above it. He also found an extra cellar on the river side of the building and on lifting a flagstone in the floor discovered a second cellar below it. Leading from here and going south towards the town was a tunnel which he ventured along for 25 yards as far as the extension lead from his light would allow. Some months later a group of archaeologists from London went further along the cramped passage but finally gave up when they came to a brick wall.

A daw (from jackdaw) is a member of the crow family alternatively known as a chough. From 1488 to 1707 the pub was known as The Cornish Chough and from 1707 to 1778 it was The Three Cornish Choughs.

Above left: The modern-day interior reflects the inn's enduring maritime tradition.

Above right: Large merchant sailing ships used to anchor up within sight of the pub while awaiting supplies and a fair wind, or on returning from long overseas voyages.

Gravesend
The Ship & Lobster

Mark Lane, Denton DA12 2QB Tel: 01474 324571

The Ship & Lobster is known as the first and last pub on the Thames. It has had several name changes from The Ship, The Chalk Wharf and The Lobster before finally becoming The Ship & Lobster in 1832. The smuggling pedigree of this ancient Thames-side tavern is impeccable. For centuries cargo ships returning from all corners of the world sailed passed its door. On occasion, either by accident or design, one would run aground on a mud bank and be stuck overnight waiting for the rising tide. This provided cover to unload illicit cargo into a snaking flotilla of small boats which stealthily emerged from the reedy margins of the river.

Charles Dickens described this historic Thames-side tavern standing 'alongside a little causeway made of stones'.

In the unlikely event of the Preventive forces spotting the activity the ship's master could claim that unloading cargo was necessary to raise the ship off the silt. Once ashore, pursuit was virtually impossible, since the low-lying land was an obstacle course of brackish pools and broad drainage dykes. Safe routes to dry land were known only to the locals.

The present-day interior of this popular pub is very comfortable but the exterior could perhaps be called scruffy – adding to its authenticity. Denton wharf was an equally scruffy industrial location in the eighteenth century when the pub was sandwiched between a windmill and a sulphur mill with tunnels beneath where contraband was secreted.

Before the sea wall was raised and strengthened the pub enjoyed a clear view of the river and its maritime traffic.

17

Today, hidden among container depots and modern jetties, The Ship & Lobster is a challenge to find but worth the effort. Although established by 1828, the pub is actually in Denton, and not listed in Gravesend directories until 1938. Charles Dickens, who knew this part of Kent intimately,

A Thames barge passes one of the numerous prison hulks moored along the lower reaches of the river.

used it as the model for the inn in *Great Expectations* where Pip hides the escaped convict Magwitch for the night, to await a ship to the continent:

'At length we descried a light and a roof, and presently afterwards ran alongside a little causeway made of stones that had been picked up hard by. Leaving the rest in the boat, I stepped ashore, and found the light to be in a window of a public-house. It was a dirty place enough, and I dare say not unknown to smuggling adventurers; but there was a good fire in the kitchen, and there were eggs and bacon to eat, and various liquors to drink. Also, there were two double-bedded rooms, "such as they were," the landlord said. No other company was in the house than the landlord, his wife, and a grizzled male creature, the "Jack" of the little causeway, who was as slimy and smeary as if he had been low-water mark too.'

In *Great Expectations* Pip is so terrified of Magwitch he agrees to help him escape.

Located on the Saxon Shore Way the pub is popular with walkers and sea anglers. There is an outside drinking area on the river wall with views of the Thames. Inside there are pictures with a nautical theme. The three changing beers normally include at least one from a Kent brewery plus one national brand and a real cider. It is advisable to book for the popular Sunday lunches and the occasional themed food nights.

Conyer Creek
The Ship Inn

Conyer Quay, Sittingbourne ME9 9HR Tel: 01795 520881

www.shipinnconyer.co.uk

A left turn off the A2 at Teynham between Sittingbourne and Faversham leads to Conyer and The Ship Inn. Despite some modern housing development this is still a lovely, lonely spot hidden away in the middle of the marshes.

By the middle ages this former Roman hamlet had developed a strong smuggling community. The Saxon Shore Way is a link of smugglers' trails which follows the coastline through here. A walk north along the creek easily shows how remote and suitable for running contraband the area would have been in the past.

This former baker's shop and blacksmith's which became a pub in 1802 has been completely renovated and extended.

Top left: There are four well-kept ales on tap including ones from local breweries.

Top right: The courtyard and garden offer panoramic views of the creek, marina and Swale marshes.

Illicit goods landed at the creek were carried inland; mixed with legitimate merchandise and sold in the market at Faversham. Larger hauls were transported to the London Turnpike, destined for the Capital. Seized goods were taken under guard to the Faversham Customs House and later sold by auction.

As well as being a traditional local the Ship is also a quality gastro pub.

On 22 March 1823 the following report appeared in the *Morning Post*: 'In the night of Saturday last a considerable seizure was made near Conyer Creek, by the men belonging to the Preventative Service stationed at Elmly Ferry; the goods taken are French silks and other fancy articles, supposed to be of nearly £10,000 value; they have been deposited at the Custom-house, Faversham.'

The building now occupied by the pub was originally a baker's shop dating to 1642 with a blacksmiths alongside. In 1802 it was owned by a Stephen Blaxland who successfully applied for an alehouse licence and called that part of the building The Ship. The other half continued as a bakery until 1831 when Sarah Beacon, a widow who had inherited the pub part, bought out the bakery and was granted a full licence for the house. In 1876 Sarah's son William sold the pub to aptly named brewer George Beer of the Star Brewery in Broad Street, Canterbury.

The Ship has subsequently been extended and very successfully renovated. It is light and airy with far-reaching views across the creek, marina and marshes of the Swale. A gastro restaurant is now the core of the business but The Ship still functions happily as a pub.

The pub is situated right on the creek and the Saxon Shore Way.

The Shipwright's Arms faces the creek so you have to enter from the car park shared with the boatyard.

Hollowshore
The Shipwright's Arms

Hollow Shore, Faversham ME13 7TU Tel: 01795 590088

www.theshipwrightsathollowshore.co.uk

As you enter this remote creek-side tavern your senses are greeted with a muted hubbub of conversation; a pleasant aroma of damp dogs, old timber, salt, tar and hoppy beer. First licensed in 1738, although much older than that, this ancient pub just oozes character.

As well as serving pirates and smugglers the inn was a well known stopping place for Thames estuary sailors and fishermen. In those days it would have been quite normal for an inn serving mariners to also provide them with 'feminine comforts'.

Built of warm brick and clad in weatherboard the Shipwright's Arms has an interior akin to a small museum. Narrow doorways lead through to small low-beamed rooms packed with interesting artifacts and evocative photographs. The classic bars are full of nooks and crannies, original standing timbers, built-in settles, well-worn sofas and a relaxed no-frills but comfortable atmosphere.

Left: If you want some ale... it had better be Goachers from the cask.

Below left: An eclectic mix of friendly characters make the pilgrimage to this remote pub.

Below right: Historical artefacts like this William III fireback continue to be revealed in the mud of the creek.

A number of items on display in the bar were recovered from the mud at low tide. These include a flintlock rifle and a Dutch cast-iron fireback of a type imported into England after the accession of William III in 1688. Dutch vessels would often sail the long way around the Isle of Sheppey to avoid detection. Contraband goods landed at Hollowshore were carried up Faversham Creek on oyster boats and openly sold below the timber-framed Guildhall in the centre of the town.

Until recently the Shipwright's Arms was self-sufficient generating its own electricity. They still draw water from their own well and use propane gas for cooking. If you make it out here during the winter you can sit around one of the four open fires.

On misty moonlit nights vast quantities of contraband were landed here.

Adjacent to the pub is Testers Boatyard, which continues the centuries-old tradition of wooden boat building. In 1860, the yard and the pub were owned by Thomas Madams. He paid £90 for the redundant prison hulk *Beresford*, which had been moored locally. After breaking it up he offered for sale through an advertisement in the *Kentish Gazette* of October 9 which read: 'Oak beams from 20 to 40 feet long, oak posts from 4 to 10 feet long, oak planks, fir beams, boards, doors, window frames &c., &c'.

Faversham
The Bear Inn

3 Market Place, Faversham ME13 7AG Tel: 01795 532668

www.bearinnfaversham.co.uk

On Tuesdays, Fridays and Saturdays the tables and chairs outside The Bear in Faversham's historic Market Place, present an excellent people-watching opportunity.

On Tuesdays, Fridays and Saturdays the tables and chairs outside The Bear in Faversham's historic Market Place, present an excellent people-watching opportunity. The market is the oldest in Kent, going back at least 900 years and the setting is well-nigh perfect, with a backdrop of beautifully kept Tudor and Georgian buildings. For centuries contraband landed at Conyer Creek and Hollowshore was openly sold here outside this ancient pub.

The light 'locals' front bar of The Bear is a late Victorian addition.

The origins of The Bear itself are lost in the mist of time. The best estimate is that the pub was probably present in the mid sixteenth century when Henry VIII's fleet lay at anchor in Faversham Creek, but it may date from as early as 1272. The scene you see today from outside The Bear has changed so little it would still be recognised by Queen Elizabeth I, who visited the town in 1572 and by Shakespeare's touring company, who acted here in 1596.

In eighteenth century Faversham experienced sailors were a constant target of Press Gangs.

HERE LIVED MICHAEL GREENWOOD, MARINER (1731/2 – 1812), WHO WAS PRESS – GANGED IN 1748, WRECKED OFF THE COAST OF MOROCCO IN 1758, AND THEN ENSLAVED BY THE MOORS FOR 17 MONTHS. AFTER BEING RANSOMED, HE RETURNED TO FAVERSHAM.

The fascia on The Bear tells us that Shepherd Neame purchased the pub in 1736. This was at the time when oyster boats carried contraband up Faversham Creek. The town's expert smuggling sailors were not only of interest to the Preventative men but also to the Royal Navy press gangs. One evening in 1748 oyster dredger Michael Greenwood was pressed in the market place – possibly after drinking in The Bear.

Ten years later he was serving in the battleship HMS *Lichfield*, with a crew of about 350, when she was wrecked off the coast of North Africa. About half the crew survived and when they came ashore were promptly enslaved by the Moors. During his captivity Greenwood kept a diary which is now in the possession of his descendants in Queensland, Australia. After seventeen months of negotiations a ransom secured the sailor's release and he returned to Faversham, settling in a sixteenth-century house at 89 Abbey Street, where he lived to be eighty.

From 1736 until 1851 regular auctions of recovered contraband – and smugglers vessels – were held at the nearby Custom House in Court Street. On 22 January 1823, during the time that Thomas Hammond was landlord of The Bear, the Customs House advertised for auction: '88 ¼ Gallons of BRANDY, 174 ½ ditto GIN, 2 pieces of FIR TIMBER, 451 HALF ANKERS, 4 ANCHORS, two WARPS. 54 FIR OARS'.

Top left: For centuries contraband landed at Conyer Creek and Hollowshore was openly sold outside The Bear. Faversham market is the oldest in Kent, going back at least 900 years.

Top right: This half-timbered, jettied house with its diamond paned latticed windows was home to mariner Michael Greenwood who was press ganged outside The Bear in 1748.

27

Today there is a relaxed atmosphere in this three-room pub. Walking down the side corridor which connects the rooms is like walking back in history. The light 'locals' front bar is late Victorian, then there's an older snug in the middle. The dining/saloon bar at the rear is the sixteenth-century part of the building. The serving bar, with an interesting frieze, also runs down the length of the pub connecting the three rooms.

Walking down the side corridor which connects the rooms is like walking back in history.

Faversham
The Anchor Inn

52 Abbey Street, Faversham ME13 7BP Tel: 01795 536471

www.anchorfaversham.co.uk

THIS ANCIENT TAVERN, FORMERLY THE ANCHOR AND STANDARD, HAS OFFERED HOSPITALITY FOR AT LEAST 300 YEARS.

A plaque on The Anchor Inn at 52 Abbey Street reads: 'This ancient tavern, formerly The Anchor and Standard has offered hospitality for at least 300 years.' The pub was probably present by 1695 and the address was earlier given as Standard Quay. Today Abbey Street is recognized as one of Britain's finest medieval streets. It was laid out as an impressive roadway to the Royal Abbey founded in 1147 by King Stephen and his wife Queen Matilda.

Top: The brown ship-lap boarded annex on the left is the coffee shop area.

This ancient tavern, formerly The Anchor & Standard, has offered hospitality for sailors from around the world for at least 300 years.

The town's famous brewing tradition dates back to this time when the Cluniac monks discovered that Faversham's pure spring water could be combined with locally-grown malting barley to produce particularly fine ale. John Caslock, the last Abbot of Faversham, was exporting beer through the town's Creek in 1525. Through the centuries, the two main commodities being smuggled out of Faversham's bustling port were wool and beer! In 1699 there were 24 breweries in the town.

The presence of an old piano adds to the comfy, pubby atmosphere of the bar.

The old inglenook is redolent of clay pipes and sea shanties.

When Daniel Defoe came here in 1724 the majority of the houses along Abbey Street and Court Street were likely to have been taverns or brothels. Writing about the massive explosion that had occurred at the Gunpowder Mill a few years earlier he said:

'I know nothing else this town is remarkable for, except the most notorious smuggling trade, carry'd on partly by the assistance of the Dutch, in their oyster-boats, and partly by other arts, in which they say, the people hereabouts are arriv'd to such a proficiency, that they are grown monstrous rich by that wicked trade; nay, even the owling trade (so they call the clandestine exporting of wool) has seem'd to be transposed from Rumney Marsh to this coast, and a great deal of it had been carry'd on between the mouth of the East-Swale and the North-Foreland.'

Tons of contraband were landed here on Faversham quay alongside legitimate cargoes.

Faversham Custom House was established in Court Street where Revenue Officers were based. They patrolled an extensive area from Milton to Whitstable, Herne Bay and Reculver. Huge quantities of siezed contraband was stored at the Custom House and later auctioned off here. *Pigot's Directory* informs us that Jesse Buesden was in charge of the Anchor from 1824 through 1840. The list of goods auctioned during Jessie's time makes interesting reading. For example: On 3 February 1824 cloth, cambrick, nankeen and 81 yards of paper hangings and, on 26 March in the same year 150 galls Brandy and 108 galls Geneva. Brandy and Gin was again for sale; on 17 January 1826 and on 17 March *The Nancy*, a 93 ton smack plus two boats, brandy and gin etc. There can hardly have been a day during the first 250 years of its existence when smuggling was not discussed or planned over a mug of Faversham ale under the roof of this ancient creek side inn.

The Custom House in Court Street where seized contraband was auctioned.

This character pub has been tastefully refurbished to retain the ancient hallmarks of the original inn. The large two-bar pub-restaurant has traditional pine boards and a brick floor with an enormous inglenook at one end and a huge wood-burner in the opposite room. The brown ship-lap boarded annex is the coffee shop area and the family-friendly establishment also has a large beer garden ideal for summer afternoons.

Seasalter
The Oyster Pearl Pub & Restaurant

(*formerly The Blue Anchor*)

185 Faversham Road, Whitstable CT5 4BJ Tel: 01227 272705

www.theoysterpearlrestaurant.com

During the eighteenth century the coast at Seasalter was an ideal spot for landing contraband. The beach consists of mud and shingle, so there was little risk of damage in beaching vessels, and open marshland backed onto the shore. The nearby Forest of Blean provided plenty of cover for the landed goods.

The former Blue Anchor, now the Oyster Pearl Pub & Restaurant, is today surrounded by caravan holiday parks.

Top: The ultra
modern interior
gives no clue to its
smuggling history.

Above: This private
house in Genesta
Avenue (nearly
opposite the more
modern 'Rose in
Bloom' pub) was
for decades the
headquarters
of the Seasalter
Company.

The contraband was brought ashore close to the Blue Anchor pub (recently renamed The Oyster Pearl) and passed on through a network of farms near the coast whose buildings benefited from cunningly-concealed compartments, windowless rooms, and secret shafts. The next stage was to move the contraband inland to Blue House Farm situated in a remote location outside of Lenham. Here heavy carts were loaded with the brandy and tobacco for onward shipment along the turnpike to the major markets in London.

The whole enterprise was highly organized and administered by a federation of ostensibly very respectable individuals operating under the innocent collective title of 'The Seasalter Company'. The Founder member was Dr Isaac Rutton of Ashford, who leased Seasalter Parsonage Farm in 1740 and used it as his headquarters.

It is now a private house in Genesta Avenue, nearly opposite the more modern Rose in Bloom pub. Rumours of smugglers tunnels were confirmed a couple of years ago when part of the back garden of Seasalter Parsonage Farm collapsed.

A letter exists, written by the corrupt Reverend Thomas Patten who was vicar of Seasalter from 1711 to 1764 and operated as a double agent informer. He lived in the vicarage which stood about 200 yards from the Blue Anchor. The letter, dated 12 March 1746, was written from Canterbury and gives a clue to the size of the gangs employed. And also how pitifully inadequate the forces of law and order were, to combat the brazen activities of such large numbers of violent men.

'On the 7th instant, a gang of about one hundred and fifty smugglers landed their cargo… and went from the sea coast about 9.0. a.m. Sixty three men and from eighty to ninety horses went by Whitstable and Faversham, and the rest went over Grove Ferry.'

The Seasalter Company flourished for over a century from 1740, and must have made many fortunes for its partners. Certainly one man, William Baldock, benefited to an unprecedented degree: when he died in 1812, he left over a million pounds – more than £200 million in today's money.

The Oyster Pearl, which stands near the point where the Faversham Road turns west to follow the sea wall along the Swale coast, is now much more of a restaurant than a pub. The ultra modern interior gives no clue to its smuggling history. Today the spot is surrounded by caravan holiday parks.

The ideal contraband landing beaches seen from the car park of the nearby 'Rose in Bloom' pub.

Whitstable
The Old Neptune

Marine Terrace, Whitstable CT5 1EJ Tel: 01227 272262

www.thepubonthebeach.co.uk

The wonky Old Neptune Inn, standing directly on the beach with no sea defences has more than once been knocked down in violent storms and rebuilt using the same timbers.

During the final decades of the eighteenth century the local newspapers in Whitstable carried regular reports of huge contraband seizures by the authorities. In the year 1788/9 no fewer than thirteen such significant seizures of goods and vessels were reported.

At this time the town had 52 pubs and a number of them (some next door to each other) stood either side of the narrow street called 'Island Wall' which was the centre of smuggling activities. Several of these properties are now private houses but still retain the original pub names including: the King's Head (No. 18), the Guinea (No. 31) and the Fisherman's Arms (No. 34). Between Island Wall and the sea, built right on the beach is the wonky 'Old Neptune Inn'.

The inn you see today is not actually as 'Old' as it appears – although the fabric is. The building has been knocked down in tempestuous storms and rebuilt several times over the years often incorporating original timbers. The warped and twisted timber structure, with its old wooden foundations, seems to accommodate movement. This can be seen in the angle of the window frames and experienced when walking across the sloping floor trying not to spill your pint.

The fact that Whitstable played a full and active part in the free trade is unsurprising, but what makes the town more unusual is its involvement in a lucrative and successful variation of the activities – the trade in smuggled prisoners of war. Between the Napoleonic War years of 1793 and 1814 enormous numbers of French POWs were brought to England, putting a considerable strain on the country's resources and leading to a vast prison building programme which included Dartmoor.

Below left: The warped and twisted timber structure seems to accommodate movement as can be seen in the angle of the floors and door frames.

Below right: The interior is cosy even when it is blowing a gale outside.

Above left: Island Wall was the centre of smuggling activities. Several of these properties still retain the original pub names.

Above right: The Fishermans Arms is one of the many former pubs in this old quarter of the town.

Many French prisoners lived in appalling conditions in filthy, overcrowded prisons and prison hulks. Relatives of the wealthier prisoners were willing to pay handsomely for their safe return. Through an elaborate network of contacts and safe havens, those who succeeded in escaping would first be brought to London. From the capital they were smuggled to Whitstable on a hoy or oyster boat before being given safe passage home to France.

This period was exceptional, though, and smuggling in Whitstable generally followed the national pattern, with smugglers moving the familiar cargoes of brandy, tobacco, lace and gin using bribery and violence.

This unpretentious weather-boarded old tavern can get very busy in the summer. It has plenty of quirky bits and pieces decorating the bar and rooms. If you don't mind your pubs being a bit scruffy, as long as they are friendly, this is for you.

Herne Bay
The Ship Inn

17 Central Parade, Herne Bay CT6 5HT Tel: 01227 366636

www.theship-hernebay.co.uk

On Easter Monday 20 April 1821 members of the North Kent Gang of smugglers rendezvoused at the home of John Richardson at Hoath, 3 miles south-east, inland of Herne Bay. Here pistols, blunderbusses and clubs (or bats) were distributed to the twenty or so men who were to form the protection guard. A further forty men were to undertake the unloading and transportation.

The Ship Inn is said to be the oldest building in Herne Bay.

Working to a pre-arranged plan devised by James West the smugglers split into a number of smaller groups and made their way by different routes to meet up by The Ship Inn. Proceeding down the beach, the fighting men fanned out in the usual style and the tub men settled down to await the arrival of the boat carrying the contraband. The night was wet and dark. About 2.45 a.m. the vessel's lights winked in answer to the signals from the beach and everything appeared to be going as planned.

OGDEN'S CIGARETTES

THE MIDSHIPMAN

Unknown to West and his men a blockade party consisting of Midshipman Sydenham Snow, Quatermaster David North and Seamen Wilson and Barker had put ashore shortly before and were proceeding on a routine patrol along the beach in the direction of the gang. Alerted by the noise of the cargo being run ashore, Snow drew his pistol and challenged the smugglers in the King's name.

Undeterred by the fusilade of shots in reply the young Midshipman pressed forward but his own pistol misfired. He drew his knife and charged but was almost immediately brought down; wounded in the shoulder and in the leg. His companions were kept at bay by the firing, unable to offer any immediate assistance.

Above: Midshipmen like Sydenham Snow were paid only £36 a year but were willing to put their life on the line to discharge their duty and earn prize money.

The successful refurbishment of the old inn reflects a nautical theme.

Ship Inn, Herne Bay

With the landing completed the smugglers made off and Snow's companions attended their wounded comrade and carried him into The Ship Inn which stood only a few yards away. He was treated by a naval surgeon from Birchington but died the following day, complaining to a comrade that it was his regret: 'That his life had not been yielded in open battle with the enemies of his country instead of being sacrificed in a vile midnight encounter with a gang of outlaws.'

The Ship Inn when Herne Bay was in its heyday as a seaside resort after the construction of the promenade and pier.

For 500 years the white painted Ship Inn stood here on the beach, serving the local fishing and smuggling community, before a group of Victorian investors from London built a pleasure pier and the promanade on which it now enjoys a central position. It is thought to be the oldest building in Herne Bay dating to around 1385. The weatherboarded extension was added around 1800 and used by military personnel from gun batteries based nearby during the period of the Napoleonic Wars.

Right: Customers enjoying the view from the newly built sun-trap terrace are protected from the wind by large glass screens.

Following a period of closure The Ship has now been completely refurbished and it re-opened in February 2010. Also in 2010 an outside decking area was added so that diners and drinkers can sit outside in a sheltered area enjoying uninterrupted sea views.

Below: A poster on the promenade in front of the Ship details the story of the smuggling era.

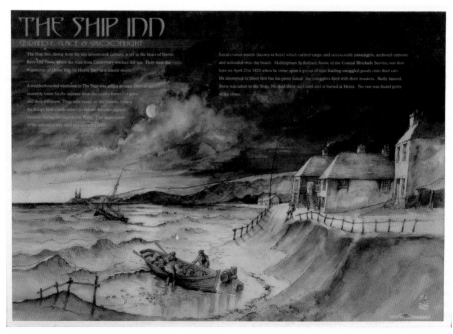

Herne Village
The Smugglers Inn

The imposing Victorian façade of The Smugglers Inn.

1 School Lane Herne, Herne Bay CT6 7AN Tel: 01227 741395

www.smugglersinnhernebay.co.uk

The Smugglers Inn stands in the centre of the village of Herne on a spot traditionally known as smuggler's corner, at the junction of Herne Street and School Lane. The building adjoins a curved terrace of half timbered smugglers' cottages and is across the road from the beautiful twelfth-century St Martin of Tours church in whose graveyard smugglers and the brave blockade Midshipman Sydenham Snow are buried.

43

Above left: The
Smugglers Inn is
a good, all-round
village local with
bar, lounge and
real fire.

Above right: The
curved terrace
of half-timbered
smugglers' cottages
adjoins the inn.
Note the lookout
window behind the
chimney stack –
shown in detail on
page 46.

On the evening of 20 April 1821 members of the North Kent
Gang were reported as having spent a considerable amount
of time at the inn. They were somewhat the worse for wear
when they left to make their way to a planned landing at
Herne Bay. Midshipman Snow, on patrol with three other
blockade men, challenged the smugglers on the beach
outside the Ship Inn and paid for it with his life.

The main road from Canterbury to Herne Bay curves round
the eastern end of the churchyard. This lovely church has
distinctive alternate bands of flint and Kentish ragstone at
the base of the tower. It is here, on the western side, that
Snow's headstone can be found – although it looks to have
been moved from its original position.

The headstone of
Midshipman Snow
on the western
side at the foot of
the church tower.

Snow was laid to rest in the churchyard here on 30 April with full military honours. His commanding officer, Captain James William McCullock (known to his men as Flogging Joey) and other officers from HMS *Severn* followed his coffin. The gunfire of the salute was heard in the pub while smugglers from the cottages opposite looked on.

Captain James William McCullock (known to his men as Flogging Joey) attended the military funeral of Midshipman Snow.

A little further up the hill from smugglers corner, set back on the left, is a building known as Box Iron House, from its original shape. When water mains were laid here in 1907, workmen came upon a honeycomb of arched cellars, approached by an interior staircase. A passage led out to the side of the road, where there was a trapdoor and chains for lowering barrels. Cellars were also discovered under the roadway itself.

A view of the pub from the churchyard in former days when it was called the Prince Albert.

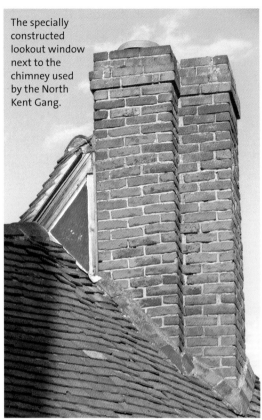

The specially constructed lookout window next to the chimney used by the North Kent Gang.

When water mains were laid under Box Iron House in 1907, workmen came upon a honeycomb of arched cellars, approached by an interior staircase.

Today The Smugglers Inn has a clean minimalist air. Darts and pool trophies have replaced the wealth of maritime exhibits that adorned the bar forty years ago. In the 1960s a store of old contraband spirit bottles was found in a hiding place behind a wall in the cellar. The chance discovery led to a more careful search which revealed a crypt-like recess in the cellar in which a number of casks, containing rum of extreme potency, were literally unearthed.

The Smugglers Inn is a good, all-round village local with bar, lounge and real fire. It has a pleasant lawned area of garden to the rear with an awning shelter and decking with tables and chairs and sun umbrellas.

Kingsgate
Captain Digby Inn

Kingsgate, Broadstairs CT10 3QH Tel: 01843 867764

www.captaindigby.co.uk

In 1769, on the sands below the Captain Digby Inn, Revenue men ambushed the much-fabled Broadstairs' smuggler Joss Snelling and his notorious 'Callis Court Gang' when they were caught in the act of landing illicit cargo. The bloody fracas that ensued here has gone down in history as 'The Battle of Botany Bay'.

Round the southern headland is Kent's best surfing beach which is commemorated as Joss Bay. In the confusion of the battle, Snelling and four accomplices escaped through an opening in the cliffs. A courageous but unfortunate Riding Officer accosted them at the cliff-top, but they shot him and fled. He was carried to the Captain Digby Inn, where he died.

The present Captain Digby Inn was developed from the stable block of the original.

On that day fifteen of Snelling's men also died. Some others who were captured were subsequently hanged at Gallows Field in Sandwich. The gang leader himself managed to escape; he had a happy knack over the years of slipping through the net. Despite the dangerous nature of his profession he managed to live for an incredible ninety-six years.

The Captain Digby has a small bar area but functions mainly as an extensive family eatery.

Below: Before cliff-face erosion the hole (seen on the right) was the entrance to a smugglers' tunnel which emerged at beach level.

The Captain Digby inn we see today has been developed from the stable block of the original which disappeared when part of the cliff collapsed in a severe storm in October 1816. Much more a restaurant than a pub, the Digby has a bar area but functions mainly as an extensive family eatery.

The inn was built by Lord Holland between 1763 and 1768 as a 'Bede House' – a place for drinking and entertainment of his guests. It is named after his nephew Robert who commanded a warship of the English fleet in 1759.

Joss Snelling lived in the adjacent village of Reading Street, where there is still plenty of evidence of the smuggling days. In 1954 contraband storage caves were revealed in the garden of a house in Elmwood Avenue when it collapsed under the weight of a bulldozer. Following the 1769 battle Revenue men mounted a search and found two dead smugglers and one mortally wounded in Rosemary Cottage in the village street.

Above left: Following the 1769 battle, Revenue men found two dead smugglers and one mortally wounded here in Rosemary Cottage.

Above right: This house in Lanthorn Road was originally the dairy to Callis Court Farm and was the home of the notorious smuggler Joss Snelling.

At a junction with Callis Court Road is Fig Tree Road. Along on the right, the house with a small copper cupola, was the 'Fig Tree Inn' and anyone seeking work as a smuggler could find it here. In 1784 the landlord eavesdropped on a conversation between officers of the 13th Light Dragoons quartered nearby and heard they were planning a raid on Deal. He sent notice by carrier pigeon to his brother who ran the Drum at Walmer (gone). Consequently, a force of 300 smugglers turned out to prevent the troops riding into the town.

Above: The former 'Fig Tree Inn' where anyone seeking work as a smuggler could find it.

Former contraband storage caves in the collapsed garden of a house in Elmwood Avenue.

Broadstairs
The Tartar Frigate

37-39 Harbour Street, Broadstairs CT10 1EU Tel: 01843 862013
www.tartarfrigate.co.uk

The eighteenth-century flint-built pub/restaurant is located at the bottom of Harbour Street.

Broadstairs was originally known by the Anglo-Saxon name of 'Bradstowe' which means 'Broad Place'. The name evolved into Broadstairs as a result of the broad 'Chapel Stairs' which once led up from the beach to St Mary's Chapel.

Visiting the area in 1723, Daniel Defoe wrote: 'Bradstow is a small fishing hamlet of some 300 souls, of which 27 follow the occupation of fishing, the rest would seem to have no visible means of support! I am told that the area is a hot bed of smuggling. When I asked if this was so, the locals did give me the notion that if I persisted in this line of enquiry some serious injury might befall my person.'

The castellated Fort House (re-named Bleak House) where Dickens stayed for a number of extended summer holidays.

Over a century later Charles Dickens came to a similar conclusion about the inactivity of the fishermen. In 'Our English Watering Place' from *Reprinted Pieces* he wrote: 'Looking at them, you would say that surely these must be the laziest boatmen in the world... Whether talking about shipping in the channel, or gruffly unbending over mugs of beer at the public-house, you would consider them the slowest men. The chances are you might stay here for ten seasons, and never see a boatman in a hurry.'

Dickens did indeed stay, on and off, for many seasons from 1837 through to 1851. During his first visit smuggling gang leader Joss Snelling was still alive. Eight years earlier Snelling had inexplicably been presented to the future Queen Victoria; introduced as 'the famous Broadstairs smuggler'. He died peacefully at the age of ninety-six in October 1837 but the smuggling tradition continued with his son, George, and his grandson.

It seems more than likely that Dickens bought some supplies from the smugglers but he also seems to have had a little unease. On 17 August 1850, his pregnant wife Catherine was confined in London. He was staying in Fort House, Broadstairs and complained to her in a letter that the Preventative men were disturbing his muse: 'I have arranged to write in the Drawing Room. I tried Georgina's room, but the Preventative men looked at me, and you know what a settler that would be to the most retiring of writers.'

'The Goblins Who Stole a Sexton' is the title of one of Dickens's Christmas stories, published with his *Pickwick Papers*. It features Gabriel Grub, a mean-hearted church sexton who is digging a grave on Christmas Eve when he is surprised by a host of goblins led by a goblin King. Grub is quizzed about the smuggled Dutch gin 'Hollands' he has been drinking.

Seafaring themes decorate the bar and dining room.

'"What have you got in that bottle?" said the goblin. "Hollands, sir" replied the sexton, trembling more than ever; for he had bought it off the smugglers, and he thought that perhaps his questioner might be in the excise department of the goblins.'

Dickens also visited the 'Tartar Frigate' during his stays and described it as: 'the cosiest little sailor's inn that is to be met around the coast... the very walls have long ago learned "Tom Bowling" and "The Bay of Biscay" by heart and would be thankful for a fresh song.'

Located practically on the beach at the bottom of Harbour Street, the Tartar Frigate takes it's name from the HMS *Tartar*, a naval ship built in the local shipyard. There has been a pub on this site since Elizabethan times but the present building dates from the eighteenth century.

The flint-built pub/restaurant occupies an idyllic position overlooking the harbour and the bay and has been the haunt of smugglers, customs men and seafarers for more than 300 years. Seafaring themes decorate the bar and dining room and there is a great seafood restaurant upstairs.

The Old Harbour Master's House stands opposite the pub.

Pegwell Bay
The Belle Vue Tavern

Pegwell Road, Ramsgate CT11 0NJ Tel: 01843 593991
www.thebellevuetavern.co.uk

In the cliffs below The Belle Vue Tavern is a small opening about 8ft above the level of the beach. This leads to 500ft of low, artificial excavations. It is called Frank Illingworth's Tunnel after the man who explored and wrote about it in 1938.

The smugglers' tunnel slopes slightly towards the sea and, before the cliff face eroded, would have emerged at beach level. During his exploration, Illingworth discovered an ancient pistol and three buttons from an Exciseman's tunic. Other tunnels connected the inn with the eighteenth-century cottages across the road.

The delightful Belle Vue Tavern dates back to at least 1760.

The terrace garden enjoys some of the best sea views to be found in Kent.

Illegal goods were cached in the tavern cellars and, in an emergency, quickly removed to cottages across the way.

Pegwell Bay on a moonlit night was the perfect landing place for the free traders contraband. The village blacksmith, known simply as 'Big Jim' ran the local smuggling gang. The luxury illegal goods were cached in the cellars of the tavern where they could be quickly removed in an emergency to the safe houses across the way.

The cliff top Belle Vue Tavern is a delightful pub with extensive views. Now owned by Shepherd Neame it was formerly a Tompson & Wotton house. It dates back to at least 1760, and in all probability, was offering accommodation, refreshment and stabling from as early as 1720.

By the beginning of the nineteenth century the inn had cleaned up its smuggling image and was receiving the patronage of royalty. In 1830 the Duchess of Kent and her daughter Princess Victoria visited the pub and its renowned tea gardens. They must have enjoyed the local shrimps served up by the then host John Cramp, for he was to receive the royal appointment as 'Purveyor of Essence of Shrimps in ordinary to Her Majesty the Queen'.

Among the many other celebrity visitors, Charles Dickens called with his family while on holiday in nearby Broadstairs, commenting: 'The shrimps were delightful, the ale better.' He also introduced children's writer Hans Christian Andersen to the delights of the Belle Vue when they visited Pegwell in 1842.

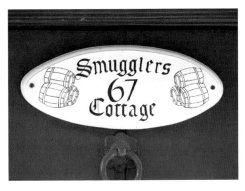

The Belle Vue was completely refurbished in early 2010 to become a well-presented pub with a contemporary restaurant. Although just a stone's throw from the busy centre of Ramsgate, it is a haven of peace and tranquillity enjoying some of the best sea views to be found in Kent.

Below: Tunnels in the cliff led up to the inn and connected with the eighteenth-century cottages across the road.

CHANNEL PORTS

Sandwich
The Kings Arms

63-65 Strand Street, Sandwich CT13 9HN Tel: 01304 617330

www.kingsarms-sandwich.co.uk

The Kings Arms stands on the corner of Church Street and Strand Street which reputedly has more old timbered houses than any other street in England.

Today Sandwich is about 2 miles from the sea, but at one time large war ships and trading vessels were able to sail up the River Stour to 'Sandwich Haven' harbour. The beach at Sandwich Bay was a favourite place for landing illicit cargoes and, in 1817, blockademen discovered a wood-lined contraband store pit here. This was one of a number of similar cleverly contrived hiding places concealed by a thick layer of shingle to defeat the use of probes.

Left: The bar is always decorated with Kentish hops.

Middle: The Royal Coat of Arms is that of Elizabeth I who visited Sandwich in 1573 and stayed opposite in the Kings Lodgings.

Bottom: Further along Strand Street from the pub is the former place of public execution.

In general rivalry did not exist between smuggling gangs. They were prepared to work together for mutual benefit but something went wrong here in Sandwich in 1746. Almost 12 tons of tea were being landed by a joint force of the Hawkhurst Gang and another band from Wingham. Before the landing was complete the Wingham men fled the scene with their share of the cargo. Incensed by this action, the ruthless Hawkhurst men gave chase brandishing their swords. In the ensuing battle seven of the Wingham men were wounded and the victors gained forty horses and most of the tea.

The Kings Arms stands on the corner of Church Street and Strand Street which is said to have more old timbered houses than any other street in England. The inn is early Tudor and was first recorded as the Queens Arms, marking a visit to the town by Elizabeth I in 1573. It was in 1687, during the reign of James II, that the inn changed its name to the Kings Arms.

This massive corner post, dated 1592, is carved into a grotesque devil crouched upon its haunches. This was one of the last earthly things condemned prisoners saw!

Gallows Field, further down Strand Street, represents the gruesome side of historic Sandwich. From the old gaol in St Peter's Street, prisoners were transported along the Strand past the Kings Arms on their way to be hung. There would have been great excitement here on the days of public executions. In 1803 people poured out of the inn and followed the procession to Gallows Field to witness the execution of eight of Joss Snelling's smuggling gang who had been captured at Kingsgate following the 'Battle of Botany Bay'.

Through the 1700s and into the 1800s the inn was a well-known coaching house and drivers and guards, acting as lookouts and informers were in the pay of smugglers from Wrotham in West Kent. The Wrotham gang could muster large numbers of horses and specialised in transporting contraband from Sandwich through Wrotham to London.

Today at the Kings Arms there is an emphasis on the accommodation and restaurant side of the business but you can still pop in for a pint. The internal appearance is just as appealing as outside And a particular feature is the original open fireplace in the bar lounge area as you enter.

Gallows Field today is part of a nature reserve established in 1970.

Deal
The Kings Head

9 Beach Street, Deal CT14 7AH Tel: 01304 368194

www.kingsheaddeal.co.uk

This handsome three-storey Georgian inn stands just across the road from the promenade and shares its seafront terrace with the Port Arms.

For a while, during the seventeenth and eighteenth centuries, the small fishing town of Deal grew to become the busiest port in England and the foremost smuggling town in the world. Ownership of the boats used for smuggling was dominated by the landlords of the seafront inns who financed the illicit trade. Every pub was a smugglers' pub.

Although never strictly a gang, the boatmen of Deal became legendary for their seamanship and for their shallow draft luggers and 40ft long galleys that held as many as 30 oarsmen. With the occasional additional boost from a small sail they could make the trip across to France in less than five hours.

Top left: The busy bar is full of interest.

Top right: The pub has a wealth of interesting maritime items and cricket paraphernalia displayed in the comfortable dimly lit areas around a central servery.

Always central to the smuggling action was the Kings Head. This handsome three storey Georgian inn stands just across the road from the promenade and shares its seafront terrace with the Port Arms. Richard Dawes was the landlord at the Kings Head on Thursday 15 January, 1784, when the beach here was the scene of the blackest day for the townsfolk of Deal.

The tiny cellar is accessed from inside the bar. The restricted space suggests it may be a small remnant of what was once a much larger storage area.

As a result of the carrier pigeon warning from the landlord of the Fig Tree Inn (see Kingsgate) 300 people were prepared and able to repel a raid by the 13th Light Dragoons from Sandwich. However, on the following day, the Dragoons were reinforced by the 38th Foot who had force marched from Canterbury.

There had been severe storms for sometime prior to this and all the Deal boats were pulled well up on the beach. Acting on the direct orders of the then Prime Minister, William Pitt the Younger, the troops moved down to the beach smashing and setting fire to the whole fleet of fishing boats and luggers. As a result of this draconian action a number of fishermen's families ended up in the workhouse.

The Three Compasses restaurant (in the foreground) was formerly a pub with a smuggling run at the top of the building allowing contraband to be spirited away through linking attics and across the rooftops of neighbouring buildings.

The burning of the boats gave Government forces only temporary relief from the activities in Deal. Soon it was business as usual. In 1801, when Richard Dawes was landlord of the Kings Head, smugglers had no trouble enlisting the help of local residents when the revenue men forced a smuggling lugger onto the town beach. The mob attacked the luckless Preventives, and brought ashore the cargo of tobacco, playing cards and bolts of fine cloth.

Until very recently miles of Deal beach resembled an untidy boatyard covered in oil, with old frame-mounted diesel engines and hawsers to pull the vessels ashore. It's tidy now but I miss the old scene.

The first mention of the Kings Head Tavern was in 1643 in relation to nearby properties.

Today the pub has a wealth of interesting maritime items displayed in the comfortable dimly lit areas around a central servery. Steps lead down directly from the bar to the cellar where contraband would have been stored.

The totally unspoilt Ship Inn is tucked away behind the seafront in Middle Street. The first reference to a building on this site was in 1694.

Deal
The Ship Inn

141 Middle Street, Deal CT14 6JZ

Tel: 01304 372222

This totally unspoilt pub is tucked away behind the seafront in Middle Street, in the very old maritime part of Deal. The interior is timeless and charmingly authentic, having retained much of its historic nautical fascination. You don't need a great deal of imagination to picture the smuggling boatmen of Deal swapping stories or singing sea shanties in the cosy back bar.

The Ship today is a tranquil haven – but it wasn't always so. In the early 1800s, after the wars with France were finally over, smuggling soared to new heights. Deal had already become the country's most notorious centre for the illicit trade and now there was a surplus of demobilized sailors moving into the town seeking profitable peacetime employment. In 1812 the pub was acquired by a retired naval sea captain called David Ross.

Right: The maritime feel of the pub is preserved with dark woodwork and pictures of local ships and shipwrecks.

An East India Man in full sail is an appropriate sign for this traditional maritime local.

During this time Revenue men faced constant danger in the town and were killed during skirmishes. Middle Street became a lawless no-go area. In its determination to combat smuggling, the Admiralty formed the Royal Navy Coast Blockade and entrusted its command to Captain James William McCulloch RN (known as flogging Joey by his men).

McCulloch vowed to restore law and order in the town and make it such a peaceable place that grass would grow in its streets. Naturally the smugglers had other ideas. They were not prepared to relinquish their profitable way of life and confrontations intensified. Major affrays reached unprecedented savagery.

On one occasion Captain McCulloch detailed two midshipmen from *The Severn* to watch a pair of boatmen in Middle Street who were suspected of handling contraband. One of the suspects, no doubt a regular at the Ship, was recognized as the notorious scoundrel Will Worthington.

The two midshipmen gave chase and pursued the men through Middle Street to Lower Street and into the Fish Market where they were surrounded by a hostile crowd who had gathered in support of the smugglers. One of the midshipmen, James Taverner, panicked and fired a shot before diving for cover in a nearby shop. Taverner was promptly arrested by the corrupt Edward Iggulsden (who was both Mayor and magistrate) and committed for trial on a capital charge. Bail was refused.

Below left: William Soames, Customs Searcher of Deal, was stabbed in the back by smugglers here in Middle Street in 1811.

On another occasion in 1818 William Soames, Customs Searcher of Deal, attempted to apprehend two boatmen who were strolling through Middle Street carrying a tub of spirits concealed in a sack. Soames gave chase and they dropped the sack but while he was examining it he was stabbed in the back with a large clasp knife.

Below right: There is a nice evening atmosphere in The Ship with candles and a woodburner in the winter.

Deal

The Royal Hotel

Beach Street, Deal CT14 6JD Tel: 01304 375555

www.theroyalhotel.com

The Royal Hotel is the only building left remaining on the beach from the many that stood side by side until the 1830s.

The Royal was originally known as the Kings Arms, but by 1699 the name had changed to the Three Kings. Today it is arguably Deal's classiest hotel but it wasn't always the case. In December 1801 Customs Officers captured a smuggling lugger near the Three Kings but as they were about to make off with their prize about 150 men stormed from the pub and retrieved the boat. A reward of £100 was offered for the apprehension of the men but it was never claimed.

Originally known as the Kings Arms, the Royal today is arguably Deal's classiest hotel.

Throughout the 1700s the pub was used as a courtroom where many a Deal boatman was tried for smuggling and for 'hovering'. The boatmen of Deal brought tea and other contraband from East Indiamen that hovered offshore in the sheltered area between the sandbanks called 'the Downs'. The shallow draft Deal lugger could negotiate the treacherous Goodwin Sands where Revenue cutters and Navy blockade ships could not give chase. It was also possible for a crew to carry a galley across the Goodwin Sands at low tide making it totally impossible for any Revenue cutter to follow.

The shallow draft Deal Lugger could negotiate the treacherous Goodwin Sands where Revenue Cutters and Navy blockade ships could not give chase.

Displayed in the Deal Maritime Museum, the Saxon King is one of only two smuggling galleys that have miraculously survived.

Deal boatmen were both heroes and villains. Some of their sea rescues were of the most heroic order but they could also be looters and traitors. During the Napoleonic Wars they smuggled out spies, French prisoners of war, letters, newspapers and gold. It was at Deal that 'Guinea boats' were constructed to smuggle out golden guineas used to pay Napoleon's troops.

On the evening of 29 July, 1801 Lord Nelson arrived in Deal to take up his position of second-in-command of the Channel Fleet. He set up his shore headquarters in the Three Kings where he had a suite of three private rooms linked by a gallery overlooking the beach. He wrote to his friends Sir William and Lady Emma Hamilton urging them to come to Deal, adding that: 'The Three Kings, I am told is the best hotel. It stands on the beach... you can bathe in the sea which will make you strong and well'.

He added that he hoped they would not be disturbed by the sound of the surf and confessed: 'I hate the Downs but if my friends come it will be paradise'. Constantly seasick, permanently cold and racked with toothache, Nelson avoided company until his mistress and her complaisant husband came to stay. Sir William spent most of his time out fishing with a reformed smuggler called Yawkins while Emma comforted Horatio.

An interesting slant on Deal in the 1700s comes from Elizabeth Carter who lived here from 1717 until 1806. Ms Carter was a prominent member of the 'Blue Stocking' group of educated intellectual women and she blamed the aristocratic customers – who should have known better – for buying the contraband: 'I hear nothing here but tea and brandy, and prohibited clothing, which is bought up with a scandalous degree of eagerness by people of fashion and fortune.'

Elizabeth was a good friend of Dr Samuel Johnson who published his famous dictionary in 1755. I wonder if it was her influence at work when he described a smuggler as: 'A wretch who, in defiance of justice and the laws, imports or exports goods as either contraband or without payment of the customs.' This seems rather hypocritical from a man who described himself as 'a hardened and shameless tea-drinker, who has, for twenty years, diluted his meals with only the infusion of this fascinating plant; whose kettle has scarcely time to cool; who with tea amuses the evening, with tea solaces the midnight, and, with tea, welcomes the morning.'

For tea drinkers in the eighteenth century it would have been impossible to avoid drinking smuggled tea. A Parliamentary Report on smuggling noted the transportation of 21,442 lbs. of tea between London and Deal over one three-month period in 1783.

In 1837 the Three Kings was refurbished and reopened under the name of The Royal Hotel in celebration of Queen Victoria's accession to the throne that year. The present day architecture suggests a build date of around 1720, replacing an earlier building, with the northern part added in the late Victorian era.

Below left: Elizabeth Carter, who lived in this house in South Street, blamed the proliferation of smuggling on the aristocratic customers who should have known better.

Below right: Dr Johnson a self-confessed "hardened and shameless tea-drinker", described a smuggler as: "a wretch who... imports or exports goods ... without payment of the customs."

Dover
The White Horse

St James Street, Dover CT16 1QF Tel: 01304 213066
www.thewhitehorsedover.co.uk

Charles Dickens, in *A Tale of two Cities*, described life in the Dover of the eighteenth century: 'A little fishing was done in the port, and a quantity of strolling about by night, and looking seaward: particularly at those times when the tide made, and was near flood. Small tradesmen, who did no business whatever, sometimes unaccountably realised large fortunes, and it was remarkable that nobody in the neighbourhood could endure a lamplighter'.

Below: The original building on this spot was erected in 1365 as accommodation for the Church-warden of neighbouring St James.

Dickens was echoing an official Customs report of 1745 which stated there were an estimated 400 men involved in smuggling in Dover with no other obvious source of income. At that time Castle Hill was the main road from Dover to Deal and below the pub were saltpans – flat areas of sea encroached land where sea water was evaporated to make salt. This is where smugglers hoards were stashed; disguised under piles of sand and scrub.

Opposite below: In 2010 the pub featured in a TV documentary about Channel swimming. During the previous decade it had become a tradition for swimmers and their support teams to sign the walls and ceiling of the bar before and after their cross-channel swims.

Modern Dover has a scarcity of ancient buildings – including smugglers pubs – because Hitler did his best to destroy them along with the rest of this ancient cinque port. The White Horse miraculously survived. St James' church, which stood next door, did not; it was destroyed by enemy shelling in 1942.

Built in 1365, the pub was originally two cottages providing accommodation for the Churchwarden of St James. With the Dissolution of the Monasteries in 1539, the church gave

Top left: The present pub dining room was used as a mortuary and inquests were held here mainly for people whose bodies had been washed up from the sea.

Top right: In the centre of the present interior there is a pair of 'exterior' doors, courtyard flagstones and a cellar entrance opening out of the carpeted floor.

OGDEN'S CIGARETTES

H.M.S. " RAMILLIES "

up the property. From 1574, for the next fifty-five years, Dover's 'ale tasters' lived here. Their duties included checking on the quality of ale and on unlawful measures.

Somewhere around 1600 William Smith bought the building and converted it into an inn. And in 1635 Nicholas Ramsey was granted permission to call the premises the 'City of Edinburgh', after a ship that sank in the Dover Straits. The pub traded for something like 200 years after that before becoming The White Horse Inn.

The fate of the infamous Aldington Gang was finally sealed here in Dover at about one o'clock on 30 July 1826. They were caught unloading tubs on the beach and, in the affray, Midshipman Quatermaster Richard Morgan from HMS *Ramillies* was killed and Seaman Michael Picket was wounded.

Midshipman Quatermaster Richard Morgan from the 74 gun ship HMS *Ramillies* was killed and Seaman Michael Picket was wounded.

Opposite: The fate of the infamous Aldington Gang was finally sealed here on Dover Beach at about one o'clock on 30 July 1826.

A reward equivalent to ten years pay for a farm labourer was offered for information leading to arrests. Subsequently George Ransley and eighteen of his men were apprehended and tried for 'being present, aiding, assisting and computing in the commission of murder.' They were all sentenced to death but the sentences were commuted and they were instead transported to Tasmania.

The White Horse today is full of character with a number of softly lit interesting rooms on different levels. It retains the original cottagey feel with curtains and nick-nacks and pastel colours. There's lots of match boarding and exposed areas of stone and brick on the walls. And a homely mix of old furniture standing on carpeted areas or old pine floor boards.

Hythe
The Bell

1 Seabrook Road, Hythe CT215 Tel: 01303 267175

The Bell was a seafront tavern in medieval times where the chimney stack was used as a look-out point accessed by steps carved inside.

Located at the east end of the town, The Bell is believed to be the oldest pub in Hythe and would have been the harbour pub when the town was a flourishing port. The original deeds to the building were lost in the days when the inn was owned by the Mackeson family, who ran the brewery in Hythe. Records of the inn that remain go back over four hundred years.

Much of the timber in this fine weatherboarded inn will have come from ships wrecked off the Romney Marsh, at a time when this site was virtually on the water's edge. Hythe's harbour was eventually closed by the build up of shingle, and pub and town were both left high and dry.

During the late 1700s most of Hythe's inhabitants were involved in the lucrative smuggling trade and traces of those turbulent times can be found at The Bell including a tunnel close to an underground mill stream which runs under the pub. Here casks of gin and brandy were stored out of harm's way, being moved by a hoist when required connected to a hook in the attic, which has survived. Another convenient hiding place was the ledges on either side of the tunnelled drain through which the mill stream flowed.

There is a gap of a barrel's width between the back-to-back fireplaces which now divide the bar and restaurant. This was a quick and convenient internal route to move smuggled goods from the cellar to the rooms upstairs. The chimney stack (seen in the picture) was also used as a lookout point. Footholds are carved into the stone and the view from the top would have given smugglers a chance to hook up barrels if the authorities were approaching. A former landlord climbed the chimney and found a clay pipe, perhaps belonging to a smuggler who enjoyed a smoke when it was his watch.

The restaurant is named after the stream that flows under the building where contraband was concealed and floated through.

A comfortably upholstered corner of the old tavern still retains its bare board flooring.

Below: One of the two back-to-back inglenooks where, in 1963, the gruesome discovery of the skeletons of two Revenue men was made.

In 1963, builder Colin Lepper, a regular at the pub made a gruesome discovery of two skeletons when he uncovered the back of the old inglenook fireplace. They were identified as being Revenue Officers because boots, belts, hats and badges had survived. All were taken to the local coroner except a couple of finger bones which were displayed in the bar for years as unusual souvenirs of the pub's history.

Today The Bell offers traditional ales; good food, comfort and more history than you could shake a sabre at. This is a smugglers' pub par excellence.

Mersham
The Farriers Arms

Mersham, Kent TN25 6NU Tel: 01233 720444

www.thefarriersarms.com

James Byham Ransley, father of the 'rascally brothers' James and William, quit Ruckinge with his family in 1792 and moved here to Mersham. The reason was possibly to be near the Hythe to Ashford turnpike which afforded potential for highway robbery; as well as for moving smuggled goods from the Romney Marsh up to London. The three Ransley girls, Anne, Mary and Elizabeth also learned to rob travellers on the high road.

Among the catalogue of their crimes at this time, father and son James were jointly charged in 1799 with armed robbery and of 'stealing eight bushels of pease... and one gallon of wheat' from Jane Austen's brother Edward Austen Knight Esquire of Godmersham Park. Although it doesn't excuse

This wonderful former farmhouse was built in the third year of the reign of Elizabeth I.

Above left: Inside is everything you would expect - beams, brickwork, boards, brass and beer.

Above right: The Ransley's curiously shaped cottage in the village of Ruckinge suggests they were never able to afford to add a second storey.

the Ransleys' crime, there can hardly have been a greater example of the haves and have-nots. Edward had inherited three great estates – each with its own mansion. He wore breeches and matching frock coats made of silk.

At the time the Ransleys moved to Mersham, John Epps and his son (also named John) owned the pub and the adjoining farriers business. The premises may have been referred to then as the 'Blacksmith's Arms'. Father and son were both known to have taken part in the brewing of ales, and at that time were probably unlicensed. Epps senior worked the forge until 1802 when his son took over the business.

In April 1806 John Epps Junior married Mary Ransley. Her rascally brothers had been hanged six years earlier at Maidstone for highway robbery. Twenty years later, there was still a connection between the pub and the Ransleys. Thomas Wheeler had possessed the property before the Epps and, in 1826 his son Thomas Junior, was convicted of smuggling and deported to Tasmania, along with other members of the Ransley gang including George, who was Mary's cousin and leader of the ruffians at that time.

In April 1799 William Ransley was convicted of an attack on the landlady of the Blue Anchor at Ruckinge and sentenced to three months hard labour which he served in Canterbury Gaol. On Thursday 24 August 1800, just a year after his release, he was publicly hanged on Peneden Heath, Maidstone along with his brother James for the crime of armed burglary.

James Ransley senior travelled to Maidstone with a cart to collect the corpses of his sons to convey them to their last and final resting place. In Ruckinge village churchyard, a hefty grave-board marks the spot where various members

of the villainous Ransley family lie buried. These included James Byham Ransley and his sons James and William, still known locally as 'the rascally brothers'.

Built in the third year of the reign of Elizabeth I, this wonderful old building was initially a farm house forming part of the estate of Simon Tindle. In 1632, whilst still in the hands of Tindle, the blacksmith's forge and stables were built. In 1828, John Epps Junior sold the house and forge to William Prebble, a farrier and common beer seller who, in 1829, was granted a licence to sell ales and ciders from a premises which he named 'The Farriers Arms'.

In 2009 the pub was about to close when 121 locals embarked on a plan to save it. They each bought a share in the pub and between them helped stump up £430,000 for the purchase of the building and an additional £200,000 to pay for the renovation. They subsequently installed their own micro brewery on the premises where they produce the popular 'Farriers 1606' Kentish Country Ale.

Top: James Ransley senior travelled to Maidstone with a cart to collect the corpses of his sons to convey them to their last and final resting place.

Above: This square brick house, which still stands at the far end of Kingsford Street in Mersham, was a step up for the Ransleys following their move from Ruckinge.

Opposite: Jane Austen's brother Edward was a victim of James and William Ransley.

Smuggling leaders Cephas Quested and George Ransley, both natives of Aldington, made the Walnut Tree their strategic headquarters.

The village sign depicts the historical local industries: smuggling, sheep farming and mining.

Aldington
The Walnut Tree Inn

Roman Road, Aldington, Kent TN25 7DT Tel: 01233 720298

www.walnuttreealdington.co.uk

The scattered village of Aldington stands on high ground overlooking the flat expanse of Romney Marsh. It would be unremarkable but for its association with the fearsome gang of smugglers known as the 'Aldington Blues'. During the early 1800s the gang operated openly and freely throughout East Kent. Aldington became their stronghold and the Walnut Tree their strategic headquarters.

The first leader of the Blues was Cephas Quested who, along with Richard Wraight, brother of the landlord of the Walnut Tree was finally captured at the 'Battle of Brookland' in 1821. Another member of the gang was wounded but made it back to the Walnut Tree and hid here successfully. Wraight was acquitted but Quested was hanged and the smugglers were left without a leader.

George Ransley, took over as leader. Born at Ruckinge in 1782, he spent his early life blamelessly as a carter and ploughman. It is said that soon after his marriage he found

Left: In the mid fifteenth century a small bedroom was added above this bar room. Reached by ladder it was used by smugglers as a lookout and signalling post.

a cache of spirits, and raised enough money from its sale to build his own house still known as the Bourne Tap. He ran this as a 'blind pig' – an unlicensed drinking den.

On July 30 1826 he and his gang were involved in an affray at Dover when Midshipman Quartermaster Richard Morgan was killed and Seaman Michael Picket was wounded. Ten weeks later, acting on information received, Bow Street Runners and Blockade officers arrived at Aldington at 3 a.m. and surprised the gang leaders in their beds. Eighteen of them were duly tried, and death sentences passed which were commuted to transportation for life to Tasmania. George Ransley was eventually pardoned, became a free settler himself, and ended his days there with the rest of his large family.

Below: This small window, high up on the southern side of the inn, is where the gang would shine a signal light to their confederates on Aldington Knoll.

The Walnut Tree still looks the part and is full of nooks and crannies and confusing passages.

Dating to the fourteenth century, the pub started life as a simple hall house and the people who farmed 10 acres that went with the property made their own cider and brewed their own beer. In the mid fifteenth century a small bedroom was added at a higher level reached by a ladder. A light set in the window could be seen as far away as the Channel coast, to provide a warning or an all clear.

The nearby Bourne Tap is the house George Ransley built from ill-gotten gains and ran as an illegal drinking den.

In 1704, the property was purchased by Jonas Quilter who was granted a licence to sell ales and ciders. In 1749 it was owned by Thomas Gadhew, who registered the title of the 'Walnut Tree'.

The pub still looks the part today; its small leaded windows and sturdy doors a match for any Excise man. Inside it is full of nooks and crannies and confusing passages. The sign depicts an Excise man, sabre in hand, coming across two smugglers at night trying to hide under a tree with their contraband.

Woodchurch
The Six Bells

Woodchurch, Kent TN26 3QQ Tel: 01233 860246

www.sixbellswoodchurch.co.uk

A big wisteria, which flowers in spring and again in summer, drapes the front of this exceedingly inviting pub.

The Diamond Family

Diamond House in Brook Street, Woodchurch is a Listed Building. English Heritage describes it as a four-bay hall house, possibly of the late fourteenth century. Following the usual detailed list of architectural features they add this caveat: 'The house was occupied by the Diamond family, a notorious family of smugglers from the late C17 to 1748, and several alcoves reputed to be smugglers' hides have been found in the house.'

During the 1740s smuggling in Kent had reached huge proportions and was heavily tainted with violence. In October 1747 the Hawkhurst Gang became involved in the audacious raid on Poole Customs House in Dorset.

Above left: The
Six Bells has a
separate public
bar and a saloon
bar with a dining
area, so there is
plenty of bar area
for drinkers.

Above right: The
middle part of the
pub is the oldest,
with different
ceiling heights
and a pleasing
confusion of
exposed beams.

Among their number that day was John (Jack) Diamond.
This incident ultimately led to the most brutal event in
smuggling history with the torture and death of potential
informer Daniel Chater and his chaperone, Customs Officer
William Galley.

Events began when a Dorset gang of smugglers suffered the
loss of a boat carrying 2 tons of tea and thirty-nine casks of
spirit from Guernsey. The confiscated goods were sent to the
Customs House at Poole and the Dorset smugglers sought
assistance from the Hawkhurst Gang to retrieve it.

The raid was successful and, on their way back to Kent,
the men from Hawkhurst crossed the River Avon at
Fordingbridge in Hampshire. At the riverside George Inn
they rested their horses, took refreshment and divided the
spoils. By the time they left large numbers of people had
gathered in the streets to cheer them on their way. One of
the townsfolk, Daniel Chater a shoemaker, recognized
Diamond and called out to him by name. The former
acquaintances had a laugh and joke and the smuggler
threw the old man a bag of tea. The Collector of Customs
for Southampton, hearing about the incident, summoned
Chater to give evidence.

Chater never made it to court, neither did Crown witness William Galley, the Customs Officer who had taken his statement and provided his escort. They were both tortured and murdered in a manner that revealed a depth of sadism, bestiality and brutality that shocked the whole nation. The smugglers had finally overstepped the mark and forfeited public tolerance. Other witnesses were found who would testify against them and the ringleaders were all hanged. There is no mention of the fate of John Diamond or reference to the family of that name in Woodchurch after that time.

The Ransley Family

The Ransley family of smugglers were also associated with Woodchurch. Following the Battle of Brookland in February 1821 and Cephas Quested's execution, George Ransley took over as leader of the last of the big smuggling gangs known as 'The Blues'. Ransley and other ring leaders of the North Kent Gang lived in the village of Aldington, but many of the foot soldiers, including Ransley family members, lived here in Woodchurch.

Ransleys lived in Woodchurch cottages for nearly three centuries from the time parish records began.

Opposite top left:
With Shepherd
Neame's rival
presence 'The
Bonny Cravat',
only a stone's
throw away, the
Six Bells remains
fiercely free.

Below right:
Diamond House in
Brook Street was
occupied by the
notorious family
of smugglers,
from the late
seventeenth
century to 1748.

Below: One of a
number of alcoves
in Diamond House
reputed to be a
smugglers hide.

In May 1826, a blockade man was killed at Camber when two hundred smugglers from the North Kent Gang clashed with Preventative forces. A few days afterwards a party of Dragoons arrived in Woodchurch looking for contraband and those involved in the fracas. A battle took place on the village green and two of the smugglers arrested were later to turn King's Evidence.

The gang's fate was finally sealed in July when they were caught unloading tubs onto the beach at Dover where Midshipman Richard Morgan from HMS *Ramillies* was fatally wounded. Although a £500 reward was offered for information no one came forward to claim it. Eventually, two other gang members captured in the earlier fighting provided the necessary intelligence.

In October 1826, acting on information received, eight men, including the leader George Ransley, were arrested in a dawn raid on Aldington. By the end of the year, eleven more of the gang had been taken. At Maidstone Assizes on Friday 12 January 1827 death sentences were pronounced on all of them. The royal prerogative of mercy was exercised and punishment commuted to transportation for life. They were all dispatched to Tasmania.

Within a few years the names of Ransley family members remaining in Woodchurch were appearing on the Pauper List. They appeared regularly in parish records of births, deaths and marriages for nearly 300 years. The first recorded marriage took place on 3 June 1703 between John Ransley and Dorothy Maxted. The last recorded was on 22 May 1976 when Stephen Thomas Ransley married his bride Angela Margaret Kirk.

The exceedingly inviting Six Bells which would have been well known to the smugglers has a big wisteria draping the front which flowers in spring and again in summer and there are benches and tables in the garden from which to enjoy it.

The middle part of the building is old, with different ceiling heights and a pleasing confusion of exposed beams. Not unsurprisingly, below the pub, are some concealed cellars not easy for a Revenue man to spot. The Six Bells has a separate public bar plus a saloon bar with a dining area, so there is plenty of bar area for drinkers.

Above right: Shoemaker Daniel Chater (John Diamond's former colleague) and Customs Officer William Galley were both tortured and murdered in a manner that revealed a depth of sadism, bestiality and brutality that shocked the whole nation.

On certain summer Sunday afternoons a battle takes place here on the large green near the pub, but today the opposing sides wear white and stop for tea half way through.

89

Warehorne
The Woolpack Inn

Church Lane, Warehorne TN26 2LL Tel: 01233 732900
www.woolpackwarehorne.co.uk

This neatly kept sixteenth-century pub restaurant is located in a lovely spot on a quiet lane near the Royal Military Canal.

In the early days of its existence in England, smuggling took the form of illegal exportation rather than importation and was directly concerned with the wool trade; England's major industry during the medieval era. The Romney Marsh was the main centre for this illegal activity and the men involved in it were known as 'owlers' because they worked stealthily by night. The inn sign of the Woolpack at Warehorne shows a couple of these characters at work with their pony and lantern.

By the Georgian period the emphasis, driven by heavy taxation, had shifted to the illegal importation of luxury goods, mainly spirits, tobacco and tea. The Woolpack at Warehorne has the greatest physical evidence of smuggling days that I have found in any pub. Inside a cupboard in the hall is the blocked up entrance to a tunnel which led directly to St Matthew's churchyard opposite. The tunnel emerges in the graveyard on the far side of the church under a cleverly constructed fake grave mound. The headstone is moveable and tilts back to reveal the tunnel exit. English Heritage attests to the authenticity of the tunnel.

Above left: Inside there is a comfortable rambling bar and spacious candlelit restaurant.

Above right: Inside a hall cupboard is the blocked up entrance to a smugglers' tunnel.

In 1817 R. H. Barham (author of the *Ingoldsby Legends*) was ordained and received the living at nearby Snargate and, at the same time, became the Curate of Warehorne. Barham famously called the Marsh the 'Fifth Continent' because he found it to be a world unto itself. He elected to live in Warehorne Parsonage with his wife Caroline whom he had married in 1814.

R. H. Barham Vicar of Snargate Curate of Warehorne and, who famously called the Marsh the 'Fifth Continent' because he found it to be a world unto itself.

Barham reported that the rustic remoteness of Warehorne was a considerable advantage to 'desperadoes engaged in what, by a technical euphemism, was termed – The Free Trade'. Naturally he learned to turn a blind eye to the smuggling activities of his parishioners. The tacit compliment was returned by the smugglers; 'notwithstanding the reckless character of these men I met with nothing of outrage or incivility at their hands.'

Many a time, on returning homewards late at night, he was challenged by a half-seen horseman who looked in the heavy gloom like some misty condensation a little more substantial than ordinary fog, but on making known his name and office, he was invariably allowed to pass on with a 'Good night, it's only parson!', while a long and shadowy line of mounted smugglers, each with his led horse laden with tubs, filed silently by.

A tombstone in the churchyard tilts to reveal the exit of the smugglers' tunnel.

Left: The stone tower of St Matthew's church (opposite the pub) was struck by lightning in 1770 and, for economy, was rebuilt in brick.

Below: Wool smugglers were known as 'owlers' because they worked by night.

Below left: The inn sign shows a couple of smugglers going about their stealthy work.

Barham wrote his *Legends* under the pseudonym of Thomas Ingoldsby and included the story of Exciseman Gill who sold his soul for a demon horse that had the ability to catch Smuggler Bill. Though it sounds unlikely, it is a rewarding read.

This neatly kept sixteenth-century pub restaurant started life as a farmhouse. It is located in a lovely spot on a quiet lane near the Royal Military Canal.

OGDEN'S CIGARETTES

THE OWLERS

Picnic sets among flower tubs overlook a meadow with beech trees. Inside there is a rambling bar with heavy beams an inglenook and a woodburner. There is modern pine furniture in the spacious candlelit restaurant which is snug with sofas and armchairs.

The Red Lion at
Snargate is not
just unspoilt; it
has remained
virtually unaltered
for over a century.

Snargate
The Red Lion

Snargate, Romney Marsh TN29 9UQ Tel: 01797 344648

www.emberpubanddining.co.uk

The Red Lion at Snargate is not just unspoilt; it has remained
virtually unaltered for over a century. That is because, for
nearly all that time, it has been in the hands of one family.
Doris Jemison was the current representative when I called,
apart from opening up a private room to provide a little
more space, she had not altered anything of consequence
since her family took over in 1911.

Nothing of
consequence has
been altered since
the Jemison family
took over in 1911.

Snargate is a remote hamlet on the western side of the Romney Marsh. It gets its name from the 'snare-gate' or sluice-gate systems used to defend the low-lying land reclaimed from the sea. The pub has been established for 450 years in this deep smuggling country. R. H. Barham (author of the *Ingoldsby Legends*) knew it well. He was Rector here from 1817 when the parish held 15 dwellings and a total population of 93 people. The parish church, a couple of hundred yards down the lane opposite, is dedicated to St Dunstan, and stands on a man-made mound, surrounded by trees.

The only way Barham, as an outsider, could function in this remote, tightknit community was to turn a blind eye to the nocturnal illicit activities of the Snargate smugglers. He couldn't ignore them because of the large cargoes of contraband tobacco stored in the church tower. This had such a pervasive odour he was able to locate the church by smell alone when travelling through the Marsh mists.

Opposite the main door, on the north wall of St Dunstan's is a faint terracotta coloured painting of a ship of around the year 1500 which was discovered under a layer of whitewash. There was a tradition on the marshes that this was an owler's coded symbol marking a place of safety.

Below left: Traditional pub games in the back bar include 'table skittles' and 'toad in the hole' which consists of pitching brass discs into the top of the commode-like piece of furniture and ringing the bell inside.

Below right: Not everything is nostalgia. The piece of sheet music on the old piano is 'Say You, Say Me' by Lionel Richie and Doris Jemison was proud to show me the visitor's book signed by Paul and Linda McCartney.

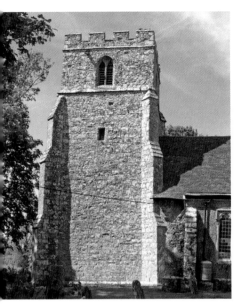

The tower of St Dunstan's church served as a contraband warehouse.

Top right: The ship depicted on this 500-year-old wall painting on the north wall of the church was adopted by the Owlers as a coded symbol marking a place of safety.

Right: The Romney or the Kent sheep is a 'longwool' sheep whose dense fleece was highly prized, leading to widespread wool smuggling.

The Red Lion is definitely not a dining pub and if Doris Jemison's legacy continues it never will be. It has a simple old-fashioned charm in three timeless little rooms with original cream wall panelling, coal fire and heavy beams in sagging ceilings. Dark pine Victorian farmhouse chairs stand on bare boards and there is an old piano stacked with books.

Local cider and four or five ales including Goachers are tapped from casks behind the unusual freestanding marble-topped counter. In the back bar there are traditional games like 'toad in the hole', 'nine men's morris' and 'table skittles'. Children are allowed in the family room, dogs in the bar and the lavatories are outside in the cottage garden.

Dymchurch
The Ship Inn

118 High Street, Dymchurch TN29 0NS Tel: 01303 874425

www.shipinndymchurch.co.uk

For six-hundred years the Ship Inn has stood defiant against the elements by the sea wall at Dymchurch.

For six-hundred years the Ship Inn has stood defiant against the elements by the sea wall at Dymchurch. Since my original visit it has undergone a complete makeover and is now a smart dining pub. When I called originally the old inn was presented largely as a smugglers' theme pub.

The present day road passes behind the Ship and the first thing I saw journeying south was the faithful reproduction of a gibbet in the garden. During the smuggling era this gruesome piece of apparatus was used to exhibit the rotting corpses of executed felons. It was designed to act as a warning and deterrent to other would be smugglers, wreckers and sheep stealers. Today it is used as a benign bracket to display the swinging pub sign.

Above: The pub sign now swings from this faithful replica of a gibbet in the pub garden.

Right: Since my original visit the old inn has undergone a complete makeover and is now a smart dining pub.

Opposite: Dymchurch beach, once the scene of contraband landings, is crowded with visitors celebrating the biennial 'Day of Syn' held over the August Bank Holiday weekend.

In the 1900s, author Russell Thorndike, brother of the famous actress Dame Sybil, was a resident of Dymchurch. Stories of the local 'free traders' captured his imagination and he wrote a series of seven novels centred on the Ship Inn where he was a regular. The pub had been a smuggler's haunt in real life and also played host to the local coroner's court, where inquests were held into the deaths of many smugglers and fishermen lost at sea.

Thorndike's fictional hero, the Reverend Doctor Christopher Syn, was the respectable vicar of Dymchurch by day; who became 'The Scarecrow' – feared leader of the 'Marsh Men' gang of smugglers by night. Thorndike had his Jekyll and Hyde preacher delivering sermons in the church of St Peter and St Paul (across the road from the pub), which has a brass plaque commemorating the author. Many gravestones and tombs in the churchyard provided inspiration for the names of his characters.

The Syn stories were several times made into films; the most notable of which is the Disney version starring Patrick McGoohan. Movie stills and Dr Syn posters decorate the reception area and there is even a 'Scarecrow Ale' by the Wychwood Brewery Company now stocked only at Halloween.

Dymchurch village celebrates its connection to Russell Thorndike and his stories by staging a 'Day of Syn' on a biennial basis held during the August Bank Holiday weekend. Re-enactments of various parts of the books can be seen at many locations throughout the village, with the 'Kings Men', 'Mr Mipps' the Sexton coffin maker and, of course, 'The Scarecrow' in attendance – it is great fun.

Above left: Actor and author Russell Thorndike creator of the Dr Syn stories seen here as Mountjoy in *Henry V*.

Above right: The Syn stories were several times made into films; the most notable of which is the Disney version starring Patrick McGoohan.

This ancient inn dates from 1410 and was originally a beacon keeper's cottage.

Below: The sign is a survival from the days when the 'woolstaplers' (wool graders) of the Weald passed this way with their laden packhorses.

Below left: The roof of the Woolpack holds out a promise to passing travellers.

Brookland
The Woolpack Inn

Brookland TN29 9TJ Tel: 01797 344321

www.woolpackinnbrookland.co.uk

When smuggling was rife on Romney Marsh the isolated location of this old treasure of a tavern, hidden down a deep lane a mile out of the village, was ideal for the clandestine activities of owlers and free traders. Today, in common with other remote rural pubs, attracting visitors is a priority. To this end, the roof is used as a giant advertising hoarding. Ten feet high white letters painted on the old red-brown Kent Peg tiles proclaim: 'WOOLPACK 15TH CENTURY INN'.

The fertile reclaimed land of the Marsh made fine grazing for hundreds of thousands of sheep, and the export of wool from their backs was for centuries both highly taxed and badly policed – almost an open invitation to smuggle. Illegal wool exports from the Marsh probably started on the day restrictions were imposed in 1275 when the government introduced a tax of £3 a bag on wool leaving England.

By 1700 up to 150,000 'packs' of wool a year were being shipped from the area days after shearing. From these beginnings the Huguenot families who controlled the trade grew into the first smuggling gangs. In 1660 wool exports were forbidden, and two years later the death penalty was introduced for smuggling. The legislators of the day probably saw this as a major deterrent, but if anything, it simply made the owlers more desperate. If you're to hang for smuggling, why hesitate to shoot your pursuer in an attempt to evade capture?

Top left: The sunken tiled floor of the entrance worn by generations of Marsh folk.

Situated both historically and geographically in the birthplace of smuggling in Southern England, the Woolpack dates from 1410 and was originally a beacon keeper's cottage and the lane is known as Beacon Lane. It has been trading as a pub for over 400 years.

Top right: Many a smugglers' conference took place in the simple quarry-tiled main bar with its massive inglenook.

Low-beamed ceilings incorporate some very early ships' timbers; maybe from the twelfth century when the sea came right up to the meadow. The beams are all pegged; no nails except some formidable handmade ones in the wattle and daub walls, some of which have been knocked down to merge all the original small rooms into one bar.

The spinning jenny mounted on the bar ceiling is thought to have been used to divide up the smuggler's spoils.

For centuries, thirsty traders would have entered the pub through the same ancient lobby you see today; with its uneven brick floor and black-painted pine-panelled walls. The Woolpack is so perfectly authentic that very little had to be altered when scenes from the Edwardian sheep-farming saga *The Loves of Joanna Godden* were filmed here in 1947.

The fifteenth-century dark oak beams confirm the pub's authenticity.

Very little had to be altered when Edwardian period scenes from *The Loves of Joanna Godden*, staring Googie Withers, were filmed here in 1947.

Located in great walking country, this is a perfect place to stop and satisfy the thirst and appetite during a day out. The pub has two large beer gardens with neat lawns, shrubs, hanging baskets, plenty of picnic-sets under parasols and a barbecue area.

The Battle of Walland Marsh

It is hard to believe today that the pretty, peaceful village of Brookland, situated between the Walland and Romney Marshes, was the scene of one of the major battles of the smuggling era. In the 1820s smuggling in East Kent was dominated by the activities of the Aldington Gang who operated along the stretch of coast between Deal and Rye under the leadership of the splendidly named Cephas Quested.

THE " BATMAN "

The customary corridor of armed men protected the others who unloaded and moved the contraband quickly on shore and inland.

Quested was an accomplished organizer who could muster hundreds of labourers from a broad area to assist in unloading a cargo. A typical run would involve up to twenty oarsmen rowing one of the long, light, galleys across from France loaded with tobacco, spirits and salt. A high speed crossing of the Channel at night could be accomplished in five hours if the tide was favourable.

On arrival, there would be a land party of two hundred or so. These comprised the customary corridor of armed men protecting the others who unloaded and moved the contraband quickly on shore and inland. On 11 February 1820, at around two thirty in the morning, just such a run was taking place at Camber Sands when the smugglers were spotted by a blockade patrol.

Within a short time a running battle began, as the smugglers retreated across Walland Marsh towards Brookland, firing repeatedly as they went. The prolonged confrontation was bloody and bitter culminating in the arrest of Cephas Quested and Joseph Wraight. They were tried at the Old Bailey on 11 April 1821. The most damning piece of evidence against Quested, which sealed his fate on the gallows, was that in the thick of the battle, he mistook a blockade man for a smuggler and handed him a pistol, suggesting that the man should 'blow an officer's brains out'. On 4 July 1821, at the age of just thirty-three, Quested was hanged at Newgate Prison.

During the year before the battle, the Royal Oak was trading as a beer house and leased to Johnathan Grist who applied for and was granted a wine and spirit licence. On the night of the fracas Grist and his family were wakened by the noise of the intense fighting in which four smugglers were killed and sixteen wounded. Midshipman McKenzie lay dead and eight other blockade men were wounded. The pub became a temporary mortuary and field hospital.

Brookland village surgeon, Ralph Pepworth Hougham, lived at Pear Tree House a few yards along the village street from the the Royal Oak. He was often called out to treat wounded from both sides in these encounters but he would be led blindfolded on horseback by the smugglers to prevent him giving them away or being asked to appear in court and give evidence on oath.

Lydd
The George Hotel

11 High Street, Lydd TN29 9AJ Tel: 01797 321710
www.thegeorgehotel-lydd.co.uk

In 1462 an ale house existed on the site of the George; almost certainly established to accommodate the masons who built the church. Cardinal Wolsey, who was rector here, raised the tower to 132 ft. high, and made the pinnacles a sign for every ship that passes down the channel.

The newly constructed George opened for business in 1620 and traded successfully as an inn for the next 243 years when it became registered as a hotel. During this time, as a staging post for London coaches, it became a meeting point for famous smuggling gangs, and was also used to hold prisoners before trial.

The church, the George Inn and the adjoining red brick Town Hall, stand in the High Street which runs along what was once a shingle bank.

The most turbulent period of the inn's history occurred during the era of the Blacklock family. When Jacob Blacklock died in 1676, it passed to his son Jeremiah who was landlord here on 7 April 1694 when a gang of smugglers attacked and ransacked many of the rooms looking for clothier William Carter. Carter, who was staying here, had published a pamphlet on the evils of smuggling and had unsuccessfully attempted to have six smugglers arrested.

In 1708 the inn passed from Jeremiah to his son Stanton who, in 1721, witnessed the biggest fracas. It became known as 'The Battle of Lydd' and took place in the inn. Jacob Walter and Thomas Bigg, smugglers from Mayfield, were taken as they came ashore from a French sloop at Dungeness. They were manacled, brought to the George and placed under armed guard. Landlord Stanton Blacklock has left us with this eye witness account:

OGDEN'S CIGARETTES

·THE FIGHT

'They was in a chamber, 6 officers with them, 20 firelocks loaded with powder and ball, at 5 o'clock on Sunday night 9 men well mounted and as well armed with pistols, swords, coopers adzes, wood bills and forks, comes up to ye house, dismounts from their horses and runs upstairs, firing all ye way. They wounded 3 officers and got between the officers and their arms and carried away Walter and Biggs; if these 9 men had not carried them off, a 100 more was hard by ready to make another attack. Jacob Walter was later recaptured by a commander in the Queens' Dragoons. The outcome of Thomas Biggs is unknown'.

When apprehended by the authorities smugglers did not hesitate to fight.

A century later, William Fisher was the innkeeper who played host to the Aldington Gang. In February 1821 Customs and Excise men had clashed with the gang at Brookland. Victims who died in the 'Battle of Brookland' and many other fights, are buried in All Saints' churchyard.

Lydd had been the most notorious of all the marsh smuggling centres; and it was here in 1829 townsfolk stood outside the George and cheered as a convoy of eighty men with twelve carts full of contraband passed through after the last major landing.

The confident little chap with the beard in the centre of this photograph looks remarkably like Joseph Conrad who lived on the Marsh and often visited Lydd.

Victims who died in the 'Battle of Brookland' and many other fights are buried in All Saints' churchyard.

Hawkhurst

Oak & Ivy

Rye Road, Cranbrook TN18 5DB Tel: 01580 753293

www.oakandivyhawkhurst.co.uk

The original part of this historic building was reputedly built in 1411. It consisted of just the right hand side of the present pub. The steep pitch of the roof indicates that it would have been a thatched hall house. The inglenook fireplace has been dated to the late seventeenth century when the pub was extended to its present size.

Built in the early 1400s the Oak & Ivy became a safe but seditious sanctuary for the biggest and most violent gang of smugglers this country has ever seen.

Opposite top: Today the Oak & Ivy has the confident lively personality of a good all-round village local. It has the unmistakable feel of a real pub – something to which people respond to instinctively.

Above: The Hawkhurst Community Partnership has established a 'Smugglers Trail' with a leaflet guide and porcelain plaques like this for the outside of the 20 participating establishments.

The inglenook fireplace has been dated to the late seventeenth century when the pub was extended to its present size.

The Civil War of the seventeenth century inspired the pub's name. In a divided country public places needed to indicate where their loyalties lay. Pubs with 'Oak' in the name, particularly the Royal Oak inclined towards support of the Royalists. Ivy was thought to kill mighty oak trees and so adding this to the name showed the pub welcomed a more Parliamentary minded clientele.

A century after the war had finished the Oak & Ivy became a safe but seditious sanctuary for the 'Hawkhurst Gang' – the biggest and most violent gang of smugglers this country has ever seen. In the absence of really effective opposition smuggling grew to massive proportions.

The process was accelerated in the early years of the eighteenth century by widespread support for the Jacobite cause who took the ivy leaf as their emblem. Smuggling was seen not just as a business transaction, but also as an act of rebellion and support for the Old Pretender. Some of the smuggling gangs openly supported the Jacobites and drank their health.

These sympathies manifested themselves in more tangible ways, too. Jacobites travelled secretly between France and England on smuggling boats and some smugglers are known to have acted as spies and double agents for the cause.

The Hawkhurst Gang hatched their plans for smuggling contraband across from France and the Channel Islands at meetings held in this pub. Their haunt was well chosen for its position on the Rye Road to London within easy reach of onward staging posts.

Further up the London Road towards the village centre stands the imposing Queen Inn. Evidence of a tunnel has been found here in the cellars.

Goudhurst
The Star & Eagle

High Street, Goudhurst TN17 1AL Tel: 01580 211512

www.starandeagle.com

This superb fifteenth-century inn and the adjacent St Mary's church stand 400 ft. above sea level commanding views across Goudhurst and the Kentish Weald. In the spring of 1747 the inn and the church played a part in one of the most curious episodes of Kent's long smuggling history.

During the Battle of Goudhurst the militia commanded the high ground here by the church and inn.

The local Hawkhurst Gang who frequented the inn, had begun terrorizing the local community. Goudhurst citizens were afraid to venture forth in the streets even in broad daylight. In April of that year, William Sturt, a soldier returned from the wars, found the villagers discussing evacuation. At this time the leader of the gang was a desperate rogue called Thomas Kingsmill, who had been raised in Goudhurst.

With a plot reminiscent of a Hollywood Western, Sturt formed a local militia to protect the townsfolk against the outlaws. Word of this initiative soon got back to Kingsmill who flew into a violent rage declaring to kill all the villagers and burn every house to the ground. He even set the deadline of 21 April for a show-down.

Sturt had only formed the militia a short time before but he straightway set about giving them basic training. Trenches were dug, barricades were built, lead musket balls were made and two hundredweight of gunpowder obtained.

At the appointed time, and true to his word, Thomas Kingsmill arrived with his gang on the edge of the village shouting insults and violent threats at the defending force. William Sturt had delivered a stirring speech to his forces and they had positioned themselves on the high ground around the inn and even on the church tower. The scene was set. Kingsmill declared that in the evening he would dine off the hearts of four of the captured villagers.

The smugglers advanced but soon found that the few days of training and preparation by an experienced soldier was more than they bargained for. Thomas Kingsmill's brother George, died from a bullet wound and at least two other smugglers were killed almost immediately in the rounds

Top left: In the attractive bar you are reminded of the days when the forests of the Weald provided England with the timber for her ships and for her homes.

Above: The Tudor dining room was formerly the kitchen.

The whole place is full of original features and provides a high level of comfort, style and character.

Below left: Skull and Crossbones crown the headstone on the grave of George Kingsmill; brother of Thomas and early fatality at the Battle of Goudhurst.

Below right: Real Ale aficionados owe a debt to the Flemish weavers who settled in these cottages by the church around 1350. They preferred 'hopped' beer to English ale and they brought with them new varieties of hops and the knowledge of how to use them in brewing.

of musket fire that were exchanged. Several others were wounded and at this point the smugglers' force was so weakened and demoralized they fled the scene with the villagers chasing them across the valley brandishing their improvised weapons.

More smugglers were wounded and several were later apprehended, tried for their crimes and hanged. William Sturt became a local hero. In a western he would have been asked to take on the role of sheriff. Instead he was appointed Master of the Goudhurst Workhouse – with accommodation for himself and his family.

The inn was originally called the 'Black Spread Eagle' and the licence dates from 1600. Bedrooms and public rooms boast original features and great character. The cellars, where contraband would have been stored, are reminiscent of medieval dungeons. Massive vaulted stonework suggests this rambling, heavily-beamed building may once have been a monastery and the tunnel from the cellars probably surfaces underneath the church.

Wrotham
The Bull Hotel

Bull Lane, Wrotham Village TN15 7RF Tel: 01732 789800
www.thebullhotel.com

Located right on the Pilgrims Way, Wrotham has always had good communications with London and the Kent coast.

During the nineteenth century, a Wrotham family became experts in 'free trade' logistics. They had a legitimate transport business, carrying goods between Sandwich and London, which served as a splendid cover for an equally successful and even more lucrative smuggling enterprise.

One member of the family, who was born around 1800, became known to his associates as 'Old Sobers'. In later life he related his reminiscences to a City businessman called John Terry who arranged to have them published. Old Sobers obviously came from a prosperous family because he told Terry: 'we could muster 50 horses'. These together with those belonging to the men of Platt and Ightham could quickly be increased to a 200 strong force, large enough to resist trouble.

Top left: The six-hundred-year-old Bull is now a smart twenty-first-century country hotel. The comfortable lounge and bar area has a timeless feel.

Top right: During WWII the Bull was frequented by fighter pilots from nearby Biggin Hill and the pub has many mementoes to the gallant few.

The family dealt in silks, lace, tobacco and spirits and had a City agent for each commodity. Old Sobers told how his father would change out of his working clothes and go in style by coach to Wood Street to meet his London merchant contacts. He also tells us how, at the age of thirteen, he would be sent at midnight in a pony trap called a 'dog cart' with a message for someone in 'the marsh'. At seventeen, he took a cart load of brooms to sell in London and returned next day with £1000. In his early twenties he went to Flushing to become the family agent and buyer there.

In 1786, a few years before Old Sobers was born, Jeremiah Shadwell took over as keeper of the Bull, leasing it from Francis Gibbon, a brewer and maltster of Wateringbury. The new landlord stayed on for thirteen years through the height of the smuggling activity. At eight o'clock on the morning of 1 June 1799, Jeremiah's brother Lieutenant Colonel Peter Shadwell of the 25th Regt of Light Dragoons pulled up outside.

He had been travelling in a curricle from Lewisham with his servant John Self en route for Maidstone, where he was Commandant of the Cavalry Depot. Outside the pub he confronted a couple of men he thought might be deserters. After questioning them he tried to apprehend them and was shot dead.

In Memory of
PETER SHADWELL,
Lieut. Col. of the 23. Regt. of Light Dragoons
and Commandant of the Cavalry Depot:
who was shot to the Heart by a Deserter
in the Public Street of Wrotham,
at 8 O'Clock in the Morning of the 1st Day
of June 1799,
in the 47th Year of his Age.

By this atrocious Deed, the Country was
deprived of a valuable Officer,
and the Soldier of a sincere Friend;
who from his extraordinary Military
Talents, rose from a Private,
to the Rank he held when Murdered.

The wall tablet in the magnificent All Saints' church Maidstone pays tribute to a valuable officer and a sincere friend.

Some sources say the forty-seven-year-old Lieutenant Colonel was the gentleman leader of the local smuggling gang but I can find no evidence to support this. Traditionally Dragoons and smugglers were arch enemies and the incident which took place outside the pub seems to suggest a devotion to duty. There is a memorial near the pub and another in All Saints' church, Maidstone where he is buried.

The plaque on the wall beside the pub marks the spot where Lieutenant Colonel Peter Shadwell was shot dead.

The eulogy in the church reads: 'By this atrocious Deed the Country was deprived of a valuable Officer and the soldier of a sincere Friend who from his extraordinary Military talents, rose from a Private to the Rank he held when Murdered.' My theory is that Jeremiah Shadwell, the pub landlord, was the smuggler and that his brother Peter's name has been forever besmirched.

Near this Place fell
Lieut Colonel SHADWELL.
who was shot to the Heart
by a Deserter on the Morning
of the First day of June 1799
The Assassin with another
Deserter his companion,
were immediately secured
and brought to Justice.

This early photograph shows that the Bull once enjoyed clear views across the countryside.

The inn first began trading under the sign of the Bull in 1385 during the reign of Richard II, and was first licensed under Henry VII in 1495. The rambling old coaching inn has undergone a labour of love refurbishment to emerge as a smart twenty-first-century country hotel.

The Vigo Inn on the summit of Wrotham Hill provided a signal point for local smugglers and a contraband storage depot. During building work a secret cupboard was discovered behind the tap room chimney.

Groombridge
The Crown Inn

The Green, Groombridge TN3 9QH Tel: 01892 864742

www.thecrowngroombridge.com

The pretty village of Groombridge with its row of tile-hung rusty coloured cottages overlooking the steeply sloping village green lies halfway between Crowborough and Tunbridge Wells. Before eventually joining the River Medway, the little River Grom flows through the village and adjoining park, defining the boundary between Kent and Sussex.

Built circa 1585 this charming tile-hung Wealden inn stands at the end of a row of pretty cottages overlooking the steep village green.

The classic bar has an inglenook and red brick floor worn uneven over centuries.

The Groombridge Gang of smugglers was also known as 'Moreton's People'. They usually landed contraband between Hastings and Pevensey also operating in the Romney Marsh area. Goods were then moved inland to be secreted in Ashdown Forest before being transported onward towards London around 40 miles north.

The gang rose to prominence in the 1730s led by Robert Moreton and John Bowra and there is an official record of their activities in 1733 when 30 of them were involved with moving tea inland from the marsh via Iden in a convoy of 50 horses.

There are corners full of interest decorated with maps and old photographs of the area.

Beers from both Kent and Sussex are on hand pump.

By 1737 the gang was said to be terrorizing the area, and the military were sent to Groombridge to restore order. In the same year an informer signing himself simply 'Goring' provided a detailed insight into the gang's activities, referring directly to an armed clash at Bulverhythe west of Hastings:

'This is the seventh time Morton's people have worked this winter, and have not lost anything but one half-hundred [weight] of tea they gave to a Dragoon and one officer they met with the first [run] of this winter.'

'...When once the Smugglers are drove from home they will soon all be taken. Note, that some say it was [Thomas] Gurr that fired first. You must well secure Cat or else your Honours will lose the man; the best way will be to send for him up to London [for trial] for he knows the whole Company, and hath been Moreton's servant two years. There were several young Chaps with the smugglers who, when taken, will soon discover [identify] the whole Company. The number was twenty-six men. Mack's horses, Moreton's and Hoak's were killed, and they lost not half their goods. They have sent for more goods, and twenty-nine horses set out from Groombridge this day... all the men well-armed with long guns.'

The neighbouring moated manor house of Groombridge Place was purchased from Chancery in 1754 by former Speldhurst bricklayer William Camfield.

At least eight of these men came from Groombridge itself including Moreton's servant Cat, Thomas Gurr (nicknamed Stick in the Mud), Collison, Pizon, Isaac Pope (Towser), John Kitchen (Flushing Jack), Thomas Ward (Bulverhythe Tom) and William Weston. In 1740 the gang was implicated in the attack at Robertsbridge on Customs Men carrying seized tea to Hastings and they continued to operate until the end of the decade, when another informer provided evidence leading to the round up and subsequent trial of the majority of the influential members.

John Bowra was apprehended and tried but acquitted. Robert Moreton continued to lead the gang including John Barbar, Thomas Nokes, Isaac Pope and William Weston until 1749 when they were betrayed by Jerome Knapp and held at Rochester until their trial. Little is known about the shadowy men who financed smuggling, but one wonders about William Camfield, a former bricklayer from Speldhurst who turned property developer during the Tunbridge Wells building boom. By 1754 he had amassed enough money to buy the Groombridge Estate which included the whole village.

The Crown Inn slips just inside Kent. Standing immediately north of the border with East Sussex it overlooks the old cottage-lined, steeply sloping village green. Demarcation was not an issue for smugglers of either county who happily collaborated in their nefarious work. Completing the row of smugglers' cottages the charming tile-hung Crown Inn, circa 1585, is screened by a row of pollarded lime trees, traditionally signalling a smuggler's safe house.

This classic Wealden inn boasts old tables and a worn red brick floor in the snug low-beamed bar. The genuine, relaxed atmosphere continues through adjoining small cosy dining rooms. A set menu and daily specials board aims to cater for all tastes. Real ales come from Kent and Sussex and Sunday Roasts are a speciality.

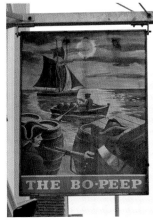

Left: The reverse side of the Bo-Peep pub sign at Bulverhythe reveals the message in the seemingly innocent nursery rhyme.

The Bo-Peep Connection

The Bo-Peep pub at Chelsfield in North Kent where the Groombridge gang handed on the booty to London gangs.

The Groombridge Gang landed goods near the Bo-Peep pub in Bulverhyth near Hastings and, employing mules or pack-ponies, transported contraband across two counties to a similarly named pub at Chelsfield in North Kent where they handed on the booty to London gangs. The Bo-Peep nursery rhyme is thought to derive from an old Hastings/ St Leonards tale and is a metaphor for the hide and seek nature of the relationship between Revenue Men and smugglers. Customs Officers were always searching and peeping while smugglers slip by carrying their contraband behind them.

THE SMUGGLERS

c. 1730, Robert Moreton (Groombridge, The Crown)

The Groombridge Gang, also known as 'Moreton's People', rose to prominence in the 1730s led by Robert Moreton and John Bowra. In 1733 thirty members of the gang were involved with moving tea inland from the marsh via Iden in a convoy of 50 horses.

c. 1740, Dr Isaac Rutton (Seasalter, Blue Anchor)

Dr Rutton from Ashford was the founder member of the 'Seasalter Company'. This innocent sounding title was used to designate a number of ostensibly respectable individuals to conceal the nature of their smuggling activities.

d. 1748, Arthur Gray (Hawkhurst, Oak & Ivy)

Arthur Gray, one of the first leaders of the notorious Hawkhurst Gang was executed in 1748 for the murder of Thomas Carswell.

d. 1749, Thomas Kingsmill (Goudhurst, Star & Eagle)

In 1748, Thomas Kingsmill took over leadership of the Hawkhurst Gang following Arthur Gray's execution. Under his leadership the gang was defeated in a pitched battle by the Goudhurst Militia. Kingsmill was executed at Tyburn in 1749 following the raid on the Customs House in Poole and the grisly murders of William Galley and Daniel Chater.

d. 1750, Gabriel Tomkins (Hawkhurst, Oak & Ivy)

Tomkins led an extraordinary life. A bricklayer from Tunbridge Wells, he rode with the Hawkhurst Gang, led the Mayfield smugglers, became a Customs Officer, went back to smuggling, was shot, arrested, jailed, transported and finally hanged in Bedford for highway robbery.

1784, Richard Daws (Deal, King's Head)

Together with other Deal publicans who were involved in smuggling, Richard Daws witnessed the devastating event of boat burning on Deal beach on 15 January 1784.

d. 1800, James & William Ransley (Mersham, Farriers Arms)

Sons of James Byham Ransley and known as 'the rascally brothers' James and William were publicly hanged on Penenden Heath, Maidstone, on 20 August 1800 – the culmination of a joint career that embraced burglary, horse stealing, smuggling, highway robbery and common assault.

d. 1817, James Byham Ransley (Ruckinge, Blue Anchor)

Patriarch of the 'Roaring Ransleys', James Byham Ransley quit Ruckinge and moved with his family to Mersham in 1792 where he died aged sixty-nine on Christmas Day.

d. 1821, Cephas Quested (Brookland, The Woolpack)

Quested, leader of the Aldington smuggling gang, was sentenced to death in 1821. He had been captured at the Battle of Brookland and accused of the murder of Midshipman McKenzie.

c. 1827, George Ransley (Aldington, Walnut Tree)

George took over leadership of the Aldington smuggling gang following Cephas Quested's death. He was transported to Tasmania with seven other members of the gang in January 1827.

d. 1837, Joss Snelling (Kingsgate, Captain Digby)

Snelling, known as 'The Broadstairs Smuggler' was born in St Peter's, Broadstairs in 1741 and, following a highly successful smuggling career, died peacefully in 1837.

d. 1890, 'Old Sobers' (Wrotham, Bull)

Son of the great smuggling family of Wrotham, Old Sobers was initiated into the wicked trade at an early age and left memoirs of his experiences.

A Smuggler's Song
by Rudyard Kipling

If you wake at midnight, and hear a horse's feet,
Don't go drawing back the blind, or looking in the street,
Them that ask no questions isn't told a lie.
Watch the wall my darling while the Gentlemen go by.

Five and twenty ponies,
Trotting through the dark —
Brandy for the Parson, 'Baccy for the Clerk.
Laces for a lady; letters for a spy,
Watch the wall my darling while the Gentlemen go by!

Running round the woodlump if you chance to find
Little barrels, roped and tarred, all full of brandy-wine,
Don't you shout to come and look, nor use 'em for your play.
Put the brishwood back again — and they'll be gone next day!

THE " FREE TRADERS "

Watch the wall my darling while the Gentlemen go by!

If you see the stable-door setting open wide;
If you see a tired horse lying down inside;
If your mother mends a coat cut about and tore;
If the lining's wet and warm – don't you ask no more!

If you meet King George's men, dressed in blue and red,
You be careful what you say, and mindful what is said.
If they call you " pretty maid," and chuck you 'neath the chin,
Don't you tell where no one is, nor yet where no one's been!

Knocks and footsteps round the house – whistles after dark –
You've no call for running out till the house-dogs bark.
Trusty's here, and Pincher's here, and see how dumb they lie
They don't fret to follow when the Gentlemen go by!

'If You do as you've been told, 'likely there's a chance,
You'll be give a dainty doll, all the way from France,
With a cap of Valenciennes, and a velvet hood –
A present from the Gentlemen, along 'o being good!

Five and twenty ponies,
Trotting through the dark –
Brandy for the Parson, 'Baccy for the Clerk.
Them that asks no questions isn't told a lie –
Watch the wall my darling while the Gentlemen go by!

BIBLIOGRAPHY

John Douch: *Smuggling – The Wicked Trade*

Steve Glover and Michael Rogers: *The Old Pubs of Deal and Walmer*

Stuart Harrison: *Customs and Smugglers in the Port of Faversham*

Wallace Harvey: *The Seasalter Company a Smuggling Fraternity*

Wallace Harvey: *Whitstable and the French Prisoners of War*

Gregory Holyoake: *Deal – Sad Smuggling Town*

Geoffrey Hufton and Elaine Baird: *The Scarecrow's Legion*

Bridget Lely: *Smuggling in Kent*

G. M. Rainbird: *Inns of Kent*

Russell Thorndike: *Doctor Syn*

D. B. Tubbs: *Kent Pubs*

Mary Waugh: *Smuggling in Kent & Sussex*